STONE HOUSES

STONE HOUSES

COLONIAL TO CONTEMPORARY

Lee Goff

Principal Photography
by Paul Rocheleau

HARRY N. ABRAMS, INC., PUBLISHERS

The Johannes Cornelius
Decker House, built in
1720–26 in Ulster County,
New York. Originally a
one-room Hudson Valley
Dutch Colonial dwelling,
it has undergone stages
of expansion.

Contents

INTRODUCTION

SINCE THE DAWN OF CIVILIZATION PEOPLE HAVE BEEN USING THE MATERIAL AT HAND to create shelter for themselves, from thatch for huts in the jungle to ice for igloos in the Arctic. Rock is the fundamental building material of the earth's crust, and it was the original material used for shelter. Neolithic peoples from Asia to Africa sought protection from the elements in rock caves and in basic houses that they built by assembling fieldstones.

"Stone, as a building material, as human hands begin upon it—stonecraft—becomes a shapely block," said Frank Lloyd Wright.[1] As civilization developed, primitive people and advanced cultures alike shaped stone to satisfy a need for artistic expression. The permanence of stone has given us a window back in time. Cairns, dolmens, and megaliths; the temples of the Maya; the pyramids of the Egyptians; Ephasus and Petra and Angkor Wat—the mysteries of ancient civilizations are revealed to us through these magnificent monuments. To build them, our predecessors used simple tools to carve, corbel, square, and stack hewn blocks, revealing colors, textures, and a beauty possible only with stone.

Wright wrote, "Each material *speaks a language* of its own."[2] A mosaic wall of stone speaks a rich visual language of texture, color, pattern, scale, and skill that cannot be found in any other material. But stone speaks a second language, an abstract one of symbol and metaphor. Stone has different moods. It can be warm or cold, protective or inhospitable. Before all else, however, stone evokes an image of power, strength, impregnability, and endurance. Even more subliminally it conveys a sense of the primordial. The rough edges of a fieldstone wall call to mind the ledges of a quarry or millenia-old outcroppings in the landscape. Instinctively, we feel the millions of years ago the stones were formed. Thus, the materials of nature become the materials of shelter, and the form the shelter takes in turn reflects the origin of the stone and the house's setting, connecting the dwelling and its inhabitants to the most permanent world of all—the natural world.

All this is true, and yet it doesn't seem enough. Not enough to explain the charisma of stone. I have contemplated the house where I have spent time in recent summers and searched in vain for a more adequate explanation for my emotional response to its stone walls. The house is in the Dordogne in southwestern France, a beautiful, hilly country of prehistoric caves, stony cliff villages, castles, churches, and châteaux built in the Middle Ages. Here stone reigns. The house's thick walls are made of the mellow honey-colored limestone that can be seen in outcroppings in the surrounding countryside. The stones, large and small, are laid in a jigsaw fitting-together held with a thick grouting of lime—a stone brocade of color, texture, size, and shape. The roof is covered in the heavy, dark gray limestone tiles called *lauzes* that are unique to the region. The materials are, as Wright said, "Nature-gifts to the sensibilities that are, again, gifts of Nature."[3] Through its materials the house grows from a landscape that has been there for millennia, long before the French and English built their embattlements and fought each other over this territory, beginning in the twelfth century. It connects me not only to the landscape but also to the people who laid the stones long ago.

But I feel something more profound, something soul-stirring for which this "stone language" alone cannot account. Finally, I can only conclude stone has the power to evoke an emotional response that goes beyond mere explanation. It is ineffable.

In North America, a land of timber, where the majority of houses are constructed of wood, there also exists a distinctive history of domestic architecture in stone. In certain regions of the country the ancient glacier left geological deposits of stone in abundance and great variety. Where there was stone, people worked it to build houses. If in the forested territory of New England you find wood dwellings, then in the rocky Wissahickon schist country of Pennsylvania, for example, you find stone houses.

Whole libraries are dedicated to architectural styles; every stylistic variation and interpretation is noted. Yet, unless it is a style primarily of stone, such as Romanesque, the materials of the style are mentioned only in passing, if at all. One may read whole chapters and not learn whether a Georgian house is brick or stone or wood. Yet, the material of a structure is essential in determining its character. Wood, for example, conveys lightness while stone, on the other hand, creates weight and durability. This is a book about one material, stone, in all its variety and its effect on the domestic architecture in which it has been used.

While stone houses make up a relatively small portion of dwellings in forest-rich America, they display a vast array of styles, methods, skills, and types of stone. This book traces the evolution of such houses from the Native-American cliff dwellings in the Southwest to handsome contemporary residences built in different parts of the country. Over the decades between, each of the architectural styles that evolved has had representations in stone. Indeed, from the earliest vernacular houses built by pioneers to the formal designs of luminaries such as Wright; McKim, Mead & White; Henry Hobson Richardson; Bruce Price and many others, the history of American architecture is not complete without a separate chapter devoted to domestic works in stone.

In an introduction to an earlier book, *Stone Built: Contemporary American Houses,* I wrote a brief history of stone houses in American architecture. I have expanded on that research for this book. The houses illustrated here were chosen to give a representation not only of various styles but also of the great variety that stone as a building material has produced.

Whether cottage or château, cabin or castle, stone houses embody feelings of romance and the picturesque. Their walls speak of permanence and history; their stones give whispered accounts of their prehistoric creation. They are an ongoing part of what Tennyson referred to as "the eternal landscape of the past."

CHAPTER 1
PREHISTORIC DWELLINGS

LONG BEFORE THE FIRST IMMIGRANTS SET FOOT ON THE SHORES OF NORTH AMERICA, the Anasazi culture built ancient cliff dwellings in the canyons and mesas of the Southwest. Archeologists have established that they were built between the tenth and fourteenth centuries. Today, the ruins of these elaborate stone dwellings can be found in national parks such as Mesa Verde in Colorado, Hovenweep in Utah, and Chaco Canyon in New Mexico. Mesa Verde alone housed hundreds of people in communal dwellings.

For some seven hundred years the pueblo culture of the Anasazi flourished in the region now comprising New Mexico, Utah, Arizona, and Colorado. They built communities first on mesa tops and later in sheltered ledges high up on canyon walls, positioned to make access difficult and, therefore, highly defensible against nomadic predatory tribes such as the Navajo.

The Anasazi, ancestors of today's Pueblo Indians, were a sedentary culture of farmers, expert at irrigating the crops they planted in the river valleys below their elevated dwellings. Their communal pattern of living, seen in the ruins, is a tradition continued by their descendants. The many kivas—the round subterranean chambers where religious ceremonies were conducted— are similar to those found in today's Pueblo communities.

According to myth, in the late thirteenth century the Anasazi simply vanished. However, archeological research indicates that after a long period of drought and a changing climate that became unfavorable, they abandoned their settlements and moved toward water. Nevertheless, mystery continues to shroud their geometrically precise fortresses. With the simplest of tools these so-called primitive people hewed thousands upon thousands of blocks of native sandstone, chipping, carving, and stacking them to form exactly squared corners and smoothly rounded towers. Built into the cliff hollows, these pueblos represent the fusion of dwelling and site that is so often a part of Indian building. The results are achievements of an ancient culture that rank with any in the world, a true architecture of stone that has lasted for centuries.

PREVIOUS SPREAD: The ruins of Spruce Tree House, Mesa Verde National Park, Colorado. The Anasazi, a sedentary culture of farmers, left the mesas to establish dwellings in high cliff hollows for defense against nomadic predatory tribes.

The ruins of Hovenweep Castle on a mesa in Hovenweep National Monument, Utah. With primitive tools the Anasazi built this smoothly rounded tower.

Anasazi kiva ruins in Chaco Canyon, New Mexico. Religious ceremonies were conducted in the round subterranean chambers.

CHAPTER 2

SEVENTEENTH & EIGHTEENTH CENTURIES

It is altogether unlikely that such words as architecture and style were
even in the vocabularies of the early settlers, much less in common usage.

—Marshall B. Davidson, *The American Heritage History of Notable American Houses*, 1971[1]

The houses built along the Atlantic seaboard during the seventeenth century and into the
eighteenth century were structures similar to the houses the early settlers had left behind.
With their steeply pitched roofs and gabled ends, they closely mirrored the asymmetrical,
informal Tudor and Jacobean houses that the colonists had occupied in the farmsteads and
modest villages of England.

NEW ENGLAND

In New England, the pioneers found stone, but it came in the form of irregularly rounded
boulders of all sizes that had been left in the wake of the ancient glaciers. They were more a
disadvantage than a welcome gift of nature. The early New Englanders struggled constantly
with the back-breaking work of moving the boulders in an attempt to clear fields for crops, as
the freeze-thaw cycle heaved more to the surface annually. Because of their round shape, the
boulders were unsuitable for house building and so were relegated to fences, walls, foundations,
and chimneys. Nature, however, made up for this burden with the gift of forests.

The majority of settlers to the Massachusetts Bay Colony were middle-class yeomen who
originated in an area of England—East Anglia—where a strong carpentry tradition was practiced. Although the region of their homeland had once been one of forests, over-cutting had
made wood scarce and increasingly expensive. Nevertheless, they had continued their tradition
of heavy-timber framing. Arriving on these shores, one can imagine the settlers' gratification at
finding themselves surrounded by a world of trees, free for the felling for lumber to duplicate
as closely as possible the medieval vernacular dwellings they had left behind. With the bounty
of New England's forests, wood was the obvious choice for houses in that region, indeed, as
it is today.

Desperate for immediate shelter, the colonists lashed together wigwams very much like
those of the Indians. But as soon as conditions allowed, they began building cottages similar to
the ones they had known in their homeland. The first winter taught them that these structures
were much too sensitive for New England temperatures, which ranged some thirty degrees more
than East Anglia. Thermal contraction and expansion opened cracks between the wood of the
exposed frame and the wattle and daub fillings (something the Indians could have told them).
The settlers realized the frame had to be wind-tight. Their solution was to cover it with shingles
or narrow weatherboarding,[2] a successful remedy that is still apparent in the surviving historic
houses of the period.

PREVIOUS SPREAD: The view from the porch of the 1720–26
Johannes Cornelius Decker House in Ulster County, New York.
The ice house was built in the nineteenth century.

THE MIDDLE COLONIES

Elsewhere along the Atlantic seaboard, in the mid-Atlantic colonies—New York, New Jersey, Delaware, Maryland, and Pennsylvania—good building stone was plentiful. Here stone was bedded in strata that broke naturally at vertical joints. Laid as it was bedded, the easily quarried material was excellent for building houses. Unlike the Massachusetts Bay colonists who came from one region of England, settlers in the mid-Atlantic region came from all over Europe, contributing to great cultural and religious diversity. The best masons were from countries with few trees such as Holland, parts of Germany, Switzerland, France, Scotland, Ireland, and areas of England. As the British carpenters of New England gloried in wood, other groups with masonry traditions seized the abundant deposits of rock to adapt to their skills. The variety of stonework that developed in the mid-Atlantic colonies was the result of differences in individual masonry skills, landscape, climate, and culture. From the sandstone of New York to the schist of Pennsylvania, the types of stone varied, and masons learned to adjust their traditions to each stone's requirements.

In addition to easily quarried surface rock, settlers used picks and axes to quarry stone that lay near the surface. For deeper deposits, they employed terracing and channeling, methods dating back to the ancient Egyptians, Greeks, and Romans. It is not surprising to find that a list of early sandstone and limestone quarries, from 1639 to about 1800, shows that most existed in areas populated with stone houses—New York, New Jersey, and Pennsylvania.[3] In the mid-Atlantic colonies, stone-house construction flourished at all levels of society.

NEW YORK

In the seventeenth and eighteenth centuries, stone was generally used in Hudson River counties from Albany County to Westchester and westward on the Mohawk River in Schenectady County. Historian Helen Wilkinson Reynolds described these houses: "The message of the stone houses . . . tells of durable material, conveniently procured under primitive conditions, which material was handled with little or no imagination or grace but with a certain inherent propriety and suitability. The stone houses, however crude, are never vulgar and almost invariably fit their setting."[4]

From 1609 until 1664, the Netherlands controlled the Hudson River Valley. In that short time Dutch entrepreneurs founded New Netherlands and established trading settlements along the Hudson River from New Amsterdam (New York City), to Fort Orange (Albany), the northernmost of the Dutch outposts. The third of these New Netherlands trading settlements was Wiltwyck, known today as Kingston, the seat of Ulster County. During the period in which the Dutch controlled the area before relinquishing it to the English—only fifty-five years—Dutch architectural expressions flourished. Traces of the colonial period are rare in New York City and Albany, but in Kingston and parts of the Hudson Valley the history of New York's Dutch colonization is quite evident.[5]

Kingston's wood houses built by the original settlers are long gone, but second-generation houses survive thanks to their materials of limestone and mortar towed from nearby fields. They stand as direct links to the Dutch settlers, their durable construction having served generations of Kingston residents.

Ulster County consists of a series of parallel mountain ranges running north and south, their valleys threaded with streams. The first settlers moving out from Kingston established their farms along the streams. Small groups formed in the valleys but were separated from one another by almost impassable mountains and wide streams. Thus, the difficulty of travel limited social contacts and contributed to Ulster County's historic conservativism.

That conservative trait is evident in many ways, one form being the standardized stone house. Indeed, the outstanding characteristic of Ulster County architecture is uniformity— of size, style, and material. The prototypical house was built in Kingston by early arrivals and then copied by those who moved from Kingston into the valleys. Similar houses continued to be built by families who remained on the same farm or in one locality for generations, handing down their traditions. New ideas were slow to penetrate and even slower to be adopted. [6]

In 1678, after the Dutch were succeeded by the British in New York, a group of French Huguenots, who had lived with Dutch families in the earlier Ulster settlement of Hurley, moved south to establish their own colony, calling it New Paltz. These French Protestants had originally sought religious freedom in Holland and then joined Dutch immigrants in coming to America like other oppressed religious groups—Puritans, Quakers, English Catholics, German Piests, and Lutherans—seeking refuge. The valley in which New Paltz lies is enclosed by ranges with outcroppings of gray rock that are severe in appearance, a harmonious setting for the Huguenots' Puritanism and moral austerity.[7] The blue sandstone, which splits easily along naturally divided vertical and horizontal joints, was ideal for the masonry skills used to build the rectangular stone houses characteristic of Ulster County.

House builders in Ulster used stone throughout the county not only during the colonial period and eighteenth century, but into the nineteenth century, long after European traditions had been assimilated into standardized construction practices. The use of stone in housebuilding declined toward the end of the eighteenth century in all the Hudson River counties except Ulster.[8]

In 1664, New York was born as a result of the Second Anglo-Dutch War. The Netherlands' direct involvement in North America ended, although in places like Kingston the influence of

Dutch architecture, as well as planning and folklife, remained.[9] The stone houses of the Dutch and the Huguenots are mainly clustered in Kingston, Hurley, and New Paltz. Some are privately owned and occupied, others are museums and may be visited.

PENNSYLVANIA

If New York offers many examples of stone dwellings, stone houses are synonymous with Pennsylvania. The area's skilled stone masons, particularly German immigrants, made use of the abundant stone deposits to construct the vernacular stone structures that are closely associated with Philadelphia, its surrounding area, and the Delaware Valley.

William Penn created Philadelphia in 1681. As a Quaker, Penn was committed to religious tolerance. He dreamed of a refuge for the persecuted, and he was determined to live in peace with the Indians, so much so that he built no city walls or fortifications. He also sought friendship with neighboring governors and with the Europeans already settled there, policies that contributed to the success of the settlement. Penn advertised the colony's attractions in pamphlets circulated in Britain and Germany. People of Germanic religious sects were particularly drawn to his ideas. They represented a major contingent of immigrants to Pennsylvania, bringing with them a masonry tradition dating back to the Roman Empire.

Indeed, hundreds of colonists came to the new settlement during the 1680s and 1690s, a heterogeneous mix of Quakers, Anglicans, Presbyterians, and Baptists. They found a climate, topography, and soil similar to that of the Old World. Philadelphia grew rapidly, becoming the social and business center of the colony, with the finest architecture.[10] Its most imposing houses were constructed of brick or stone. In addition, the city's surrounding rich farmland attracted

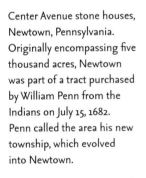

Center Avenue stone houses, Newtown, Pennsylvania. Originally encompassing five thousand acres, Newtown was part of a tract purchased by William Penn from the Indians on July 15, 1682. Penn called the area his new township, which evolved into Newtown.

numbers of Germanic and Swiss settlers. Stone was the material favored by the Germanic gentry who developed a strong local tradition of sturdy fieldstone structures reflecting the medieval styles of northern Europe. They also contributed the practical bank-sited barn, with its cold room dug into the slope for food preservation.

EIGHTEENTH CENTURY

By the eighteenth century, the American colonies had become a rapidly growing outpost of the British Empire. The practice of building on the basis of tradition and using the materials at hand in response to the local environment progressed to a more cosmopolitan architecture concerned with matters of style. Colonial eyes were fixed on the current architectural modes in England and the fashions of London society.

During that period, Philadelphia was the main port of entry for thousands of immigrants, some of whom came for religious freedom, most for economic gain. As a result, Philadelphia grew rapidly as a mercantile and shipping center. A middle class developed to influence not only social, cultural, and commercial affairs, but architectural styles as well. The architecture of England became the architecture of America, although it took several years to make the crossing and then was subject to the interpretations of local builders.

GEORGIAN STYLE

From the early 1700s until the Revolution, the Georgian style popular in England dominated the American colonies. Based on the classical design principles of the Italian Renaissance and the designs of the Italian architect Andrea Palladio (1508–1580), the symmetry, formality, and dignity of this British style represented a final break with the earlier asymmetrical and informal Tudor architecture. Unlike houses of the seventeenth century, Georgian houses were symmetrical; their ceilings were uniformly high; their formal planning centered the fireplace between doors, which were capped with broken pediments. British pattern books provided builders with measured drawings of classical details, and the wave of masons and craftsmen emigrating from England helped to develop and spread Georgian design principles in America.

The professional architect had not yet appeared in the colonies. Most designers were amateurs, well-to-do gentlemen with the leisure to read and study pattern books and architectural theory. Their reliance on Renaissance principles and Palladio's designs resulted in Georgian houses along the Atlantic seaboard having a uniformity that did not exist among the houses of the seventeenth century. From the most imposing mansions of wealthy New England seaport traders to the plantations of gentlemen farmers in the South, from the manor houses of bankers' estates in New England or New York to simple and modest backcountry farmhouses, the Georgian style was widely adopted.

Some regional variations in Georgian houses did exist and were based on local materials and social attitudes. Strong local traditions of Swedish, German, and Welsh Quaker builders, for example, combined the Georgian style with their own vernacular. While Germanic groups were responsible for folk architecture in the farm country surrounding Philadelphia, another large contingent came from the midlands of England where, unlike their New England brethren, they were accustomed to masonry construction. They are thought to be responsible for the pent, although it is also attributed to Germanic settlers. A distinctive feature of Pennsylvania houses of the period, the pent is an eave mounted above the first-floor door and windows, sometimes extending the length of the house.[11]

FEDERAL

Although the Revolution brought about a break with England, post-Revolutionary American architecture continued to follow British fashions. After the Revolution, the proportions of the Georgian house began to be refined. The neoclassical movement that had developed in Europe in the mid-eighteenth century was making an impact in America by 1790, where it evolved into two distinct styles: the Federal style, lasting approximately from 1790 to the 1820s, and the Greek Revival style, from 1820 to 1860.

Still rooted in the Classical orders, the Federal style differed from Georgian design in concepts of proportion, scale, and the delicacy of ornament, which was adopted from decorative elements such as swags and garlands that were associated with the work of influential English architect Robert Adam. The Federal mode in design began as one primarily of the Federalist aristocracy, but was eventually adopted everywhere in vernacular forms. Its most common application was in brick or frame dwellings. However, choice of material was dominated by local availability, and many Federal mansions were constructed of limestone and other local stone.

With the end of the Revolution, people began to feel that architecture in the new United States should be symbolic of the new nation. As a sense of American identity grew, so did the demand for architecture of the common man as well as the privileged. In his influential builder's guide, *The American Builder's Companion: or a New System of Architecture Particularly Adapted to the Present Style of Building in the United States of America* (Boston, 1806), Asher Benjamin asserted that with different materials, less use for decoration, and a need to economize on labor and materials, architecture in America must be different from that of Europe. The goal was to bring comfort, dignity, and quality to all classes.[12]

HENRY WHITFIELD HOUSE
GUILFORD, CONNECTICUT 1639

A rare exception to colonial-era wood construction in New England was the stone house built in 1639 in Guilford, Connecticut, for the Puritan separatist Reverend Henry Whitfield. While the house's form is that of the later Tudor and Jacobean buildings of England—asymmetrical, with small casement windows, immense chimney stacks, a steeply pitched roof, and gabled ends—it resembles cottages from the north of England rather than the yeomans' cottages in Whitfield's home area of Surrey and Kent. A distinctive difference is the external chimney stack that is typical of Cotswold cottages. This difference may have been due to the influence of William Leete, one of the few settlers from the north of England who came with Whitfield. An aggressive leader, Leete later became governor of Connecticut.

The stone house was constructed not only as a residence for Henry Whitfield and his family, but also as a stronghold for the community should King Charles I's forces pursue them to enforce the oppressive rule of the Church of England from which they had fled. They perhaps chose to build the house of stone for the fortified protection that wood could not provide. The granite gneiss used for the building was quarried from a ledge about a quarter of a mile away, and tradition has it that friendly Indians helped the settlers transport it on hand barrows. They mixed yellow clay and crushed oyster shells to make mortar for the house's two-foot-thick walls. The new settlers had not yet learned from New England winters to make their rooms small for easier heating, thus they built a Great Hall (thirty-three by fifteen feet).

The house stands today as a house museum, faithfully restored with subsequent alterations removed. As the oldest known stone house in New England, it is not only an exception to the predominant wood construction of the region, but also evidence of the durability of stone.

Built in 1639, this is the oldest known stone house in New England. It served not only as a residence for Reverend Henry Whitfield but also as a community stronghold against the King's troops seeking to enforce the oppressive rule of the Church of England from which Whitfield and his fellow settlers had fled.

The Great Hall, with its massive hearth measuring more than ten feet in width. The Governor William Leete chair in the foreground is an outstanding example of American seventeenth-century furniture.

Diamond-pane casement windows
illuminate the upstairs bedroom.

In 1678, a group of French Huguenot families settled the area of Ulster County, New York, that would be called New Paltz. They moved south from the earlier settlement of Hurley where they had lived with Dutch families. Old records refer to the houses they built as "medieval Flemish" architecture, but it is more accurately called Hudson Valley Dutch vernacular. Recent research by the Huguenot Historical Society indicates that the houses date from the late 1680s, rather than 1694 as earlier thought. Most of the houses started as three-room dwellings constructed of local fieldstone, the stones, in hand-portable sizes, laid one upon the other just as they were taken from their bedding. Some slabs were larger than others, making walls two feet thick, which led to a structural innovation: beams and joists could be laid directly on the walls, thus eliminating vertical posts, an example of vernacular adaptation.

Although the houses pictured here bear a general resemblance to each other, they vary in detail. All were started at the same time. However, Jean Hasbrouck's house—something of an anomaly with its steeply pitched roof, immense open attic, and square dimensions—is much more barnlike and rural in feeling than Abraham Hasbrouck's, which is more urban. Although the Bevier-Elting house also belonged to a French Huguenot, more than the others it shows Dutch influence. Its gable end faces the street, a characteristic of Dutch urban houses and unique on Huguenot Street.

The Jean Hasbrouck house was for many years the society's only property opened as a museum. Its contents interpret three hundred years of life in Ulster County.

ABOVE: The divided door in the kitchen of the Bevier–Elting house allows in fresh air and welcome sunlight.

OPPOSITE: Solid shutters and a double transom above the split door are characteristic of the early Hudson River houses built by the Dutch, whose architecture influenced the French Huguenot settlers.

LEFT: Like other houses in the New Paltz settlement, the Bevier–Elting house started as a three-room field-stone dwelling and was subsequently enlarged. The west room, facing the street, was the living space. The adult cradle, used by an elderly bedridden member of the family, is positioned in what was probably the warmest part of the room.

OPPOSITE: A five-plate stove or "jamb stove" in the kitchen would have been positioned up against this heat passage so that wood could be fed into it from the adjacent parlor. This is a rare surviving feature since most such openings were subsequently filled in.

OPPOSITE: With its steeply pitched roof, immense open attic, and square dimensions, the 1694 Jean Hasbrouck house resembles a barn, in contrast to the other Huguenot houses. The wooden gable above the tie beam is a typical Dutch element.

LEFT: The Bevier–Elting kitchen fireplace is an enclosed English type with remnants of a small bake oven.

The tavern room of the Jean Hasbrouck house. Begun in the late 1680s, the house is believed to have attained its current form by 1712. Home to five generations of Hasbroucks and later tenants, a general store with a tavern operated here. The hanging scales date from 1746, and an early liquor license hangs above the mantel.

The Jean Hasbrouck house has walls of
local fieldstone that are two-and-a-half
feet thick. Old records refer to its
architecture as "medieval Flemish," but
it is more accurately termed Hudson
Valley Dutch vernacular.

The kitchen of the Jean Hasbrouck house includes an eighteenth-century green-painted Windsor chair and a slat-back chair next to an eighteenth-century table. The material culture displayed in the house reflects three hundred years of history in the New Paltz area.

The Gomez Mill House is the oldest surviving Jewish homestead in North America. Located near Newburgh, New York, the house has been inhabited continuously for more than 280 years. Built on the site of an ancient Indian ceremonial ground, operated as a frontier trading post, and used as center of patriot activity during the American Revolution, the Mill House was intertwined with events of early American history.

In 1714, Luis Moses Gomez, fleeing from the Spanish Inquisition, obtained a grant from Queen Anne allowing him to purchase six thousand acres of land on the Hudson River Highlands where several Indian trails converged. The Queen also granted him the right to trade with the Indians. Gomez built a fieldstone house into the side of a hill near a stream that became known as "Jews Creek." The old Indian trail leading to the Hudson River winds past the front gate to the house. Across from it is the spring where Indians stopped to drink; today it still provides water to the house.

Of the original house, little has changed. The walls are three feet thick. The split doors, the heavy beams, and the massive door posts and lintels remain. Facing each other at opposite ends of the living room are two great fireplaces. One has an oven behind it that is big enough for a month's supply of bread. Two cellars were originally built into the hillside, one of which was used to store pelts brought by the Indians for trading.

Before the Revolutionary War, Gomez sold Mill House to Wolfert Acker, a Dutch American who added a second story and attic to the house using bricks made from local clay. Although the material is different, the addition continues the solidity and dignity of Gomez's original house. Acker became a lieutenant in the New Marlborough Company of Minute Men, and his company held secret meetings for the new patriots at Mill House.

In 1979, descendants of Luis Moses Gomez and of subsequent owners formed the Gomez Foundation for Mill House to preserve the house as a unique historic Jewish home.

LEFT: An old Indian trail leading to the Hudson River winds past the gate of the Gomez Mill House.

OPPOSITE: The Gomez Mill House is the oldest surviving Jewish homestead in North America.

ABOVE: Little has changed of the original house. The split doors, the heavy beams, two great fireplaces, and massive door posts and lintels remain.

OPPOSITE: The thickness of the walls—three feet—can be seen at the door jamb. On the table at the right is an antique menorah.

ABOVE: Before the Revolutionary War, Gomez sold the house to Wolfert Acker, a Dutch-American who added a second story and attic to the house using bricks made from local clay.

OPPOSITE: The gable end of the house shows the stonework of the original house and the second-story brick addition.

In 1664, the Dutch lost control of the Hudson River valley to the English. However, the architecture of the earlier settlers continued to have an influence, as can be seen in this 1730 house in the Dutch Colonial style, built for Cornelis Van Buren. Now owned by renowned jockey Billy Pearson and his wife Margaret, it is an outstanding example of Kingston's collection of Dutch stone houses.

Tobias Van Buren had built his own house a block away before building this house for his son, Cornelis. Size and number of rooms were indications of class in the seventeenth and eighteenth centuries, so the house's two stories suggest that the owner was a member of the wealthy merchant class. Father and son were traders with the Indians, dealing in beaver pelts that they tanned in the tannery behind the house for the coats, hats, and collars that were the height of fashion in Europe at the time. A cousin, Martin Van Buren, was eighth president of the United States.

During his long riding career, Pearson, in addition to collecting stables full of racing trophies, has collected and refurbished houses—seventeen of them. Only the fifth owner of this house since 1730, Pearson had lived in the Netherlands for eight and a half years before moving to New York State. It is by coincidence that he and his wife purchased a Dutch Colonial house, discovering only after they acquired it that Kingston began as a Dutch settlement.

The Pearsons have brought together in this residence their collection of primitive and folk art and painted furniture, which they have acquired over a fifty-year period. Imbued with history, the house provides an appropriate setting for these objects.

The living room of the house contains pieces from Billy Pearson's folk-art collection. At the far left corner of the room is a painted German dowry armoire from 1834. Between the windows is a carved Napoleonic prisoner-of-war armchair. The folk-art coffee table has a nineteenth-century prison-made tabletop.

In a bedroom, an American pencil-point tiger-maple campaign bed, painted blue.

Though constructed in 1730 after the Dutch lost control of the Hudson River Valley, this house shows the continuing architectural influence of the Dutch colonists.

OPPOSITE: The view into the living room from the entrance foyer. The drop-leaf table is an eighteenth-century Swedish example.

ABOVE: The tiger-maple banister is original to the house.

In the 1730s, a few English Quakers from Chester and Darby, Pennsylvania, established a settlement at Wright's Ferry, in wild and virtually uninhabited country along the Susquehanna River. Susanna Wright, the original owner of Wright's Ferry Mansion, was a dynamic force in the settlement. Known as "the bluestocking of the Susquehanna," she had links with England and Philadelphia. Her interests and knowledge were astonishingly wide. She was proficient in French, Latin, and Italian and studied some of the local Indian dialects. She brought European literature to the colonists, as well as knowledge of medicine and law. Neighbors came to her for advice as well as healing. She corresponded with Benjamin Franklin, and they exchanged small gifts. And if all this were not enough to occupy her, Susanna established a thriving silk industry, supplying prizewinning silk to the Queen for the birthday celebration of George III.

Like the 1738 Wright's Ferry Mansion, the Georgian houses in Pennsylvania, New York, and New Jersey were predominantly built of stone. The style of this house is vernacular Georgian with the addition of the pent or eave above the first-floor windows and doors, a regional feature introduced by Pennsylvania Germans.

Restored by the von Hess Foundation and furnished to the time of Susanna's ownership, the house is imbued with English Quaker grace and simplicity. Its spare furnishings exhibit the restrained elegance and sophistication of Philadelphia William and Mary and Queen Anne work. The austerity of bare, wide plank floors serves to emphasize the beauty of the collection of furnishings, one of the most complete and representative from the period 1700 to 1750 in the country. The house presents a trove of academic information within the atmosphere of early-eighteenth-century American culture and aspirations.

Wright's Ferry Mansion contains one of the country's most complete and representative collections of American artifacts from the first half of the eighteenth century, some of which are seen here in the kitchen.

OPPOSITE: The entrance hall, showing the double transom and Dutch door.

Susanna Wright built this Pennsylvania Georgian-style house in 1738 on the Susquehanna River. The eave above the first-floor windows, called a pent, is a vernacular feature common in Pennsylvania.

The bedroom, like the rest of the
house, is furnished to the time of its
original owner.

The restrained elegance and sophistication of the Philadelphia William and
Mary and Queen Anne furnishings are
accentuated by the austerity of bare
wide-plank floors and windows without curtains.

One of the finest examples in stone of the Georgian mode is Benjamin Chew's house, Cliveden. Built in the 1760s as a country house in Philadelphia's Germantown section, its history spans seven generations of Chews.

The house's symmetrical facade—with its pediments, modillions, and flared lintels with keystones—exhibits the characteristic neoclassical details of the Georgian style. The mason responsible for the house's stonework exaggerated its three stories by laying progressively thinner courses of dressed stones from foundation to roof. Five carved-stone urns imported from England crown the roof, an exuberant touch for a city of Quaker sensibilities and a tradition of understated elegance. The sober exterior cladding of gray-brown local schist and unornamented keystones offset such ostentation.

One hundred years after Benjamin Chew built the house, Anne Penn Chew, Cliveden's late-nineteenth-century owner, revived it after a period of decline and built a two-story addition to the rear, employing rubble stone matching that of the original rear elevation.

The house was the scene of the Revolutionary War's Battle of Germantown, during which a contingent of about one hundred British soldiers, marched on by General Washington, took shelter in Cliveden, barricading themselves behind its thick stone walls. Washington ordered an assault on the house. The symmetrically aligned windows allowed cannonballs fired by American troops to pass through Cliveden's front and rear windows, striking American troops on the other side with friendly fire.

In a city that was once the world's second-largest English-speaking city and for a time capital of the nation, where so many sites have historical associations, Cliveden survives as a handsome expression of colonial architecture. One of the eighteen house museums operated by the National Trust for Historic Preservation, Cliveden is interpreted by its curators in ways that connect it to its people—men and women, children, servants, and slaves who lived there—as well as put it in context as an outstanding example of Georgian architecture in stone.

Cliveden, which takes its name from the country house of Frederick, Prince of Wales, is one of the finest examples in stone of the neoclassical Georgian style. The house's symmetrical facade displays the pediments, modillions, and flared lintels with keystones that are the style's characteristic details.

ABOVE: The dependencies at the rear contain a kitchen and a laundry.

RIGHT: Cliveden's stone barn is built into a hillside and includes a room dug into the hill for cold storage. Its masonry is executed in a manner that is typical of vernacular stone architecture in Pennsylvania.

CHAPTER 3

NINETEENTH CENTURY

Stone is generally conceded to be superior, on the whole, to any other material for building. This is owing to its great durability and solidity, both in expression and in reality.

—Andrew Jackson Downing, 1842[1]

ROMANTICISM AND THE PICTURESQUE

By the 1820s a broad popular culture was developing, and Jacksonian America—optimistic, idealistic, and expansive—had an extravagant admiration for faraway Greece and its associations with democracy. Greek temples seemed imbued with romanticism. Characterized by qualities of serenity and dignity, their forms swept the nation, undoubtedly as much for their ease of adaptation and reproduction as for their ideological appeal.

Although the temples that inspired the style were of monumental stone, they were generally interpreted in America in wood and painted a pristine white. Based on the post-and-beam construction of Greek temples, the structural method of the Greek Revival had much in common with Georgian and Federal architecture, as did the reliance on classical design principles, although now those of Greece rather than of Rome. Greek style houses—rectangles with their gables turned to the street—multiplied. Turning the gable to the street produced the form of a pediment that, if extended forward, could rest on columns to create a porch. The gable-fronted house with a great columned portico was the shining example. But the Greek Revival mode filtered down to the most modest rural houses—simple, rectangular masses with applied Greek detail. Where stone was easily quarried and used, the interpretation was more expressive.

In the years when Texas, Kansas, Iowa, and Minnesota opened to settlement, the nation's population grew from 10 million to 31 million and the western boundary met the Pacific.[2] Whether wood, brick, or stone, Greek Revival was the fashion. Its influence can be seen today throughout the country on thousands of neighborhood streets, whether in freestanding residences or rowhouses. Soon enough, however, the pendulum of architectural fashion would swing in the opposite direction. Although Greek Revival was the first of the romantic styles, a quite different romanticism was to replace it.

The Revolution had brought an end to the relative simplicity of colonial life, and by the turn of the nineteenth century a more diverse culture was rapidly developing. The guarantees of the Constitution encouraged individual freedom and a break with the established conventions of colonial society. At the same time, the works of artists and writers made people aware of the vastness and beauty of the American continent.

Romanticism, which gave birth to the phenomenon of the picturesque, had come to America from Europe at the close of the eighteenth century. Nostalgia for a remote time and place as well as a reverence for the beauty of untamed nature are hallmarks of the Romantic movement. The

PREVIOUS PAGE: The Centre Family Dwelling, a Shaker dormitory structure in Pleasant Hill, Kentucky, has paired entrances for the Brothers and Sisters.

appeal was to the emotions rather than to the mind, thus Romanticism was quickly embraced by an expanding young society in search of forms expressive of the uniqueness of the nation. Picturesque architecture in the romantic mode, dynamic and lively, appealed to the increasingly individualistic tendencies of society. Unlike the whiteness and smoothness of classic architecture, picturesque styles were intended to show a patina of age; they were irregular, their textures rough, and their colors rich, warm, and dark.[3] Indeed, the very description of stone.

Throughout the nineteenth century both romanticism and advancing scientific and technical knowledge were forces behind the conquest of the wilderness on one hand and the development of architecture on the other.[4] As the population of America increased, migrant groups in search of more land and greater opportunity dispersed into the vast unsettled territories between the Appalachian Mountains and the Mississippi River and beyond. They adapted and varied their Old World masonry traditions and experience to the dictates of geography, the local stone, and climate as well as social and economic factors. The differences and peculiarities of the various styles that resulted were a response to circumstances rather than to the whims of fashion. Necessity and convenience produced a perfect architectural expression of their individual conditions and needs. Because of the enduring quality of stone, now, more than a century and a half later, many of these regional vernacular houses live on, of interest to today's architects because of their particular genius for practical solutions.

With an influx of expert artisans, masonry attained a level of excellence. Local stone and the techniques of the various artisans contributed to the character of regional vernacular dwellings such as the cobblestone houses of upstate New York, the German stone houses of the Texas Hill Country, the limestone buildings of Wisconsin and Minnesota, and the fieldstone houses of Pennsylvania. While none of this vernacular work constitutes an architectural movement, it is a testament to the ingenuity and artistry of these craftsmen.

As pioneers were venturing into new territories, American cities were expanding. Prior to about 1840, local quarries and glacial deposits were able to meet the demand for stone, and it was seldom shipped great distances. But by mid-century rail and shipping lines had webbed their way into the nether regions of the country, and new waves of immigrants brought growing numbers of skilled masons and a supply of cheap labor. If the early settlers had initiated stone construction, it proliferated as stone was shipped wherever it was wanted. And it was indeed wanted for the houses of a rapidly growing, prosperous mercantile class, as entrepreneurs called on builders and the new profession of architects for houses that would be manifestations of their status, wealth, and taste. In the pageant of nineteenth-century Victorian styles, stone in all its variety was a leading building material. Gothic Revival, Italianate, Second Empire, Queen Anne, Romanesque, Tudor Revival—the styles nipped at each other's heels, the features of one overlapping those of the next. With the Romantic enthusiasm for nature and the picturesque styles—characterized by texture, irregularity, variety, polychromy, intricacy—stone construction was in demand.[5]

As the century progressed, the names of architectural titans became attached to important domestic stone architecture. Among them were Richard Morris Hunt, McKim, Mead & White, Henry Hobson Richardson, and A. J. Davis. Alexander Jackson Davis's pattern books for villas and cottages, published in the 1830s and 1840s, greatly influenced the picturesque movement. His books differed from earlier builders' guides in that they showed how a house should be shaped rather than merely how it should be detailed. Davis deplored American domestic architecture and its classical styles, particularly their lack of connection to the site. Interest in how a building related to its natural setting made the use of stone inevitable. Revivals of polychrome, irregular European styles such as Gothic and Italianate swept away the order, balance, and whiteness of the Greek Revival. Brownstone was well suited to the brooding quality of these picturesque styles and was used in urban town houses and large country villas as well as in the cottages that came to be designed for the middle class.

In 1838 Davis met Andrew Jackson Downing, an architectural critic and landscape designer. Between 1840 and 1875, Davis's architecture and Downing's writings dictated fashion in American domestic architecture. Downing wrote that not only should the landscape be planned to enhance the house, the house should be designed to relate to its setting: "Architectural beauty must be considered conjointly with the beauty of the landscape or situation."[6] In his early books, Downing advocated building in stone for its naturalistic and historical qualities. He opposed the imitation of stone forms in wood: "When we employ stone as a building material, let it be clearly expressed: when we employ wood, there should be no less frankness in avowing the material,"[7] a dictum that would be restated in the twentieth century by Frank Lloyd Wright. Although Downing was forced to adjust to using more easily obtained and economical wood, especially for his smaller cottages, he did not completely give up his feeling for stone. He disliked white paint, finding it much too glaring against the soft green of foliage. Instead, he proposed a palette in "shades of gray . . . and . . . drab or fawn color, which will be found pleasing and harmonious in any section of the country."[8] At least one could have the shades of stone, if not the material itself.

A stone house in Chester, Vermont.

For the mansions of the rich along the Hudson River, stone became the fashion, something Downing approved. "A mansion may very properly have a graver color than a cottage, to be in unison with its greater dignity and extent," he decreed.[9] Victorian authors compared the scenery of the Hudson River to that of the Rhine. To America's new wealthy class, the notion of their own castles on the American Rhine was seductive. They built local versions of English Gothic manor houses, French châteaux, and castellated mansions. John Zukowsky describes them: "Such rough-hewn stone villas with tall towers and flared roofs . . . were in keeping with Downing's recommendations for 'Rhenish' villas appropriate to typical Hudson River sites. Castellated mansions with their heavy masonry and forbidding parapets were not only evocative of ruins along the Rhine but, one might say, befitting of the robber baron status of some of their owners."[10] Chateauesque mansions were built until about 1910 when once again architectural fashion turned to classicism.

The late 1850s and the 1860s saw the decline of Gothic Revival and Italianate, to be replaced in turn by French-inspired Second Empire, English-inspired Queen Anne and Tudor, and Romanesque, styles that employed stone—carved and rusticated, ashlar and rubble—to expressive effect.

The greatest figure in architecture in the 1870s and 1880s was Henry Hobson Richardson (1838–1886). His reputation as America's most original architect was rivaled only by that of Frank Lloyd Wright in the following century. Influenced by his training at the prestigious Ecole des Beaux-Arts in Paris, Richardson's work showed a new sense of planning, opening the separate interior spaces to each other. Rather than simply a circulation area, the hall became an open and informal living area featuring entrance, fireplace, and stairs. In what would become known as the Shingle Style, he emphasized the new interior continuity by sheathing the exterior surface with a shingle covering that wrapped smoothly around corners, towers, and over roofs in one continuous envelope. Stonework was often used in foundations and chimneys, sometimes even for the entire first floor, grounding the house firmly to its site. Adapting medieval European architecture, Richardson interpreted the interior planning and the exterior forms—the towers and turrets and arches—in such an innovative way as to create a truly American style. Indeed, by the end of his career, Richardson had eliminated nearly all specific historical references in his buildings, emphasizing mass and proportion.

At the same time that he was designing wood structures in the Shingle Style, Richardson was also designing masonry structures in the Romanesque Revival style, a mode of great power, simplicity, and sculptural beauty based upon the textures of stone. Highly personal, his bold designs for magnificent public buildings, churches, and private homes came to be known as Richardsonian Romanesque. The outstanding characteristics were massive, rusticated ashlar stonework and half-round arches that sprung forcefully from their bases. His residences in this style—formal, weighty, fortress-like—offered their occupants the sense of security that their position and assets seemed to require.

Richardson's work had a significant influence throughout the country. But, expensive to build, the style was short-lived and declined in the 1890s.

As the popularity of the Romanesque style faded and the Victorian era came to a close, architects began to reject the picturesque styles. The 1893 World's Columbian Exposition in Chicago marked the beginning of a new interest in classicism, regenerating the kind of formal order, symmetry, and whiteness that had gone out with the Greek Revival. From the Revolution until the end of the nineteenth century, architectural styles went through swings of fashion from informal, colonial vernacular to formal classicism and back to the informal picturesque. Now, on the eve of the twentieth century, the pendulum was about to swing back to classicism.

DESHON–ALLYN HOUSE
NEW LONDON, CONNECTICUT 1829

The late Federal style Deshon–Allyn House was constructed in New London, Connecticut, in 1829, at a time when the Greek Revival style was reaching a fever pitch of popularity in the nation. The original owner was Daniel Deshon, a successful merchant, who later sold the house to Lyman Allyn, a prominent New London whaling captain. Built at a time when the town was a prosperous whaling port, the house is vernacular Federal in character, but with little of the ornament of that style, while also incorporating Greek Revival details.

The exterior of the ten-room house is constructed in local rubble granite, unusual in a region where wood houses predominate. The unknown architect-mason may have used Asher Benjamin's influential 1806 builder's guide to reinterpret, in stone, details intended for a frame house. For example, elements such as the door and window surrounds are ponderous granite posts and lintels, details that would have been more appropriate in wood. The lintels also lack the keystones and splayed ends of the Federal vocabulary. The Palladian window is a motif that belonged to the Georgian period but was sometimes found in vernacular Federal dwellings in areas of New England. And, while the elevation's entablature is in the Palladian Doric order rather than a Greek order, Greek Revival influence can be seen in the use of a flat transom light, rather than a Federal fanlight, over the door. However, it is in the interior where the Greek Revival style dominates. The woodwork displays what was then the latest thing in elegant Greek detail.

As a house museum open to the public, the interior has been restored and richly furnished to approximate its 1829 appearance.[11]

The Deshon–Allyn House was built in 1829 for Daniel Deshon. Stucco or some other material may have been intended to face the rubble stone walls of the exterior, which is Federal in character. The design was probably influenced by Asher Benjamin's builder's guide. The Palladian window, although associated with the earlier Georgian period, was sometimes found in vernacular New England Federal dwellings.

ABOVE: The furnishings in the south parlor are from the nineteenth century. The English sofa, circa 1810, has gold and black painted decoration. Flanking it are 1870s armchairs in the style of Duncan Phyfe. The marble-topped mahogany pier table between the windows was made in Providence, Rhode Island, circa 1830. On it is an American whale-oil lamp from about 1840.

OPPOSITE: The mahogany dining table with carved ball-and-claw legs dates from about 1840. The side chairs are from a set of six made about 1815. An English girandole mirror from the same period hangs above a sideboard with ormolu mounts, dating from 1825.

In the 1830s and 1840s many Shaker families with the means to do so built large residences in anticipation of an influx of converts. Of such dormitory houses, the Centre Family Dwelling was one of the largest and most impressive. The facade gives little indication of the structure's more than forty rooms and just over 24,000 square feet. Fifty-five by sixty feet with a 140-foot ell at the rear, the dwelling is the largest building constructed in Pleasant Hill's Shaker community.

White limestone, known locally as "Kentucky Marble," was quarried nearby and laid in regular courses. Built at the height of Greek Revival's popularity, the style is nevertheless Georgian, or more accurately, as a regional example of Shaker architecture, "Georgian Shaker." The building includes Greek Revival and Federal details prevalent in Kentucky and the South at the time. Also typical of regional features is the T-plan, containing a large kitchen, which was used in all Shaker Village's bigger structures. Regional too are the double doors for the Brothers and

Sisters. Many other Shaker dormitory dwellings had a single entrance with separate steps.

Ten years in construction, the dwelling's walls were erected in 1824, but due to upheavals in the community further building was delayed and the structure was not completed until 1834. When the Centre Family finally moved into their new home, they numbered a hundred members. The Brothers and Sisters occupied dormitory-style sleeping quarters on several floors and shared a thirty-four-by-eighty-five-foot dining room.

Within the context of Shaker strictures, the building made use of some rather "worldly" decoration—columns and wainscoting in the dining room, a curved ceiling and plastered cornice in the meeting room. The blend of style and ornament makes this a unique Shaker structure. Worldly as the design may be, Shaker simplicity prevails, making the Centre Family Dwelling all the more beautiful for it.

LEFT: The columns and paneled wainscoting in the dining room were somewhat "worldly" decorative elements within the context of Shaker simplicity.

OPPOSITE: The Centre Family Dwelling was built in two phases, in 1824 and 1834. It is constructed of white limestone, known locally as "Kentucky Marble." The facade gives little indication of the structure's 24,000 square feet, though it has oversized proportions: the doors are ten feet high and the second-floor windows, seven feet.

OPPOSITE: The floors are made of ash and oak with a natural finish. The high ceilings help to keep the building cool in summer. The spare interior beautifully expresses the Shaker aesthetic.

ABOVE: The Centre Family Dwelling is a regional example of Shaker architecture. It includes an eclectic blend of elements from various styles that were prevalent in Kentucky and the South at the time of construction.

The greatest concentration of cobblestone houses is found within a sixty-mile radius of Rochester, New York, where the practice originated. The first such house was built in the vicinity of Lake Ontario in the 1820s. The art of cobblestone building, which continued for the next forty years, spread south to the Finger Lakes region and west as far as the Illinois-Wisconsin border. Said to have been initiated by immigrant masons who had worked on the Erie Canal in the 1810s, the basic form was a Greek Revival gabled rectangle, with many houses in later years acquiring Gothic Revival or Italianate Victorian details and additions.

Uniform, water-rounded stones, gathered from the lakeshore or riverbeds, were carefully graded for their color, shape, and size and laid up with distinctive mortaring. Masons shaped the mortar into raised tri-angles or pyramids, or molded it into V-shaped or rounded joints to create intricate patterns, such as herringbone or honeycomb, that set off each stone like a gem in its individual box. Corners were finished with dressed limestone quoins. The mass of the wall was usually fieldstone rubble, sometimes brick, with the cobblestone applied as a veneer. The work was slow, painstaking, and impressively creative.

Like other regional vernacular stone houses, the cobblestone houses of upstate New York constitute a valuable collection of folk architecture. Within one generation, nearly one thousand cobblestone houses were built in Greek Revival and Victorian styles. As many as nine hundred such structures survive in New York alone. In demonstrating so imaginative a use of their material, the cobblestone houses have a unique charm.

The Barone house in LeRoy, New York, is Greek Revival in style, though its gable is uncharacteristically turned away from the street.

The Rippley house in Seneca, New
York, reveals a Victorian influence in
its bracketed eaves and fanciful door
surround.

OPPOSITE: The arched windows and gable detail of the Rippley house are characteristic of the Queen Anne style.

A detail of the Rippley house's decorative stonework. The water-rounded stones of the cobblestone veneer were taken from lakes and riverbeds and carefully graded for uniformity.

The Hawks house is a Gothic Revival example of the cobblestone vernacular. Many such houses are said to have been built by masons who worked on the Erie Canal.

In 1846, the first wagon train of 120 settlers arrived in what was to become the town of Fredericksburg, Texas, future seat of Gillespie County, in the heart of the Texas Hill Country. One of a projected series of settlements, Fredericksburg was laid out like the German villages along the Rhine from where many of the colonists had come. The German Immigration Company, which controlled ten thousand acres of the Texas land, granted each of the first arrivals one Townlot (100 by 200 feet) for a house and one ten-acre Outlot for farming.

While at first the terrain seemed lush with green grass, the settlers soon found that within a season or two wind and rain eroded what was a thin, fragile layer of soil. Just below lay chalky limestone, less conducive to crops perhaps, but certainly good for house building. The settlers used their masonry skills to construct the stone houses that today, a hundred and fifty years later, are still solid and orderly in contrast to much of the area's ramshackle scenery.

The early houses reflect the masonry skill of the immigrants—a skill dating back to the time of the Romans—as well as the simple rectangular house forms they brought from Germany. As time went on Victorian details found vernacular interpretations, such as intersecting gables and other picturesque details, but the basic form remains.

Religion was an important part of the lives of the German settlers of Gillespie County. On weekends they drove considerable distances for religious services, and so they used their town lots to build houses for overnight stays, known as Fredericksburg's Sunday houses.

Today, Fredericksburg has developed into a popular destination with restaurants, motels, art galleries, and antique stores. Various annual events attract visitors. The town's historic stone houses have been preserved, many of them restored for use as vacation houses and second homes.

Additions, visible at the left in this
photograph, have expanded the
Reder house.

The living room of the Reder house has an exposed interior wall of Hill Country limestone.

Built in 1849, the Kammalah house in Fredericksburg is among the earliest of the German rock houses.

A Fredericksburg Sunday house.

The Fassel Roeder house, a typical Hill
Country house built in 1858.

The kitchen of the Fassel Roeder
house has limestone walls.

When the owner of this limestone spring house in the Hill Country of Texas decided to restore and renovate it, he insisted first and foremost that the architects, John Grable and Javier Huerta of the San Antonio firm of Lake/Flato, respect the integrity and spirit of the original mid-nineteenth-century house, as well as the history of those who were there before the house was built.

The original dwelling was two stories high and one room deep with a second section connected by a dogtrot (or breezeway), a Southwestern vernacular element. Built in 1852, at a time when white settlers still intruded on the Comanche tribes, the house is fortresslike. A fifty-five-degree spring flowing from a nearby hillside fed a water course that ran under the house, providing a source of water and refrigeration. This also endowed the inhabitants with a primitive form of comfort in a hot climate.

Restoration research began with old photographs, according to John Grable. Over the years, additions had been made to the original structure. A saddleback added to the rear of the house blocked light and cross ventilation; removing it exposed views of the surrounding terrain and the flowing spring water, which had been contained by a previous owner in a stone-lined acequia.

The addition of a new two-story front porch was justified when, in the process of restoration, its original beam openings were found. The central stair in the dogtrot was relocated, revealing a door and reestab-lishing the front-to-rear axis. Its new upstairs landing gives access to two bedrooms, a bath, and the second-floor porch. The acequia flows directly under the dogtrot in an enclosed tunnel. All duct work for mechanical-system upgrading, such as electrical and air conditioning, had to be hidden. Lighting is kept to the level of kerosene lamplight.

With the main house renovation established, client and architects constructed at the rear of the house an outdoor cooking porch, fireplace, and barbecue pit of stone gathered from the site. Grable describes this as an ode to former use since most houses had outdoor kitchens. Another connection to place and history was the contribution of second- and third-generation German and Mexican craftsmen from the area, who were as inventive as their forebears had been in addressing the many problems encountered.

Finally, a stone guest house was constructed across the acequia from the cooking porch, thus creating a courtyard. Modern amenities such as stereo, television, and computer are contained in this subservient structure, as well as a laundry room.

The renovation of this ranch house was one of restraint, allowing the architecture to speak for itself. The respectful treatment of the dwelling's original form honors its historic and cultural precedents, and is very much in the tradition of Lake/Flato's philosophy of integrating art and science to merge building and landscape.

LEFT: All modern technology, such as computers, television, and stereo, has been exiled to the guest house.

OPPOSITE: According to project architect John Grable of Lake/Flato, "The goal was to protect the integrity of the house, to do as little as possible. The site and view prompted the second-floor porch to be added. Openings for the original porch beams were found during restoration, justifying its replacement."

Originally, most houses in the region had outdoor kitchens. The porch, fireplace, and barbecue are an ode to the former use of the structure. In the background is the guest house.

The guest house defines the back
courtyard space, tying the site together.
A subservient element, its spare treatment serves to emphasize the importance of the main house.

The removal of a saddleback (or shed) at the rear of the one-room-deep house uncovered a view of the hills and provided cross ventilation. Spring water flowing under the house is contained in a stone-lined acequia built by a previous owner.

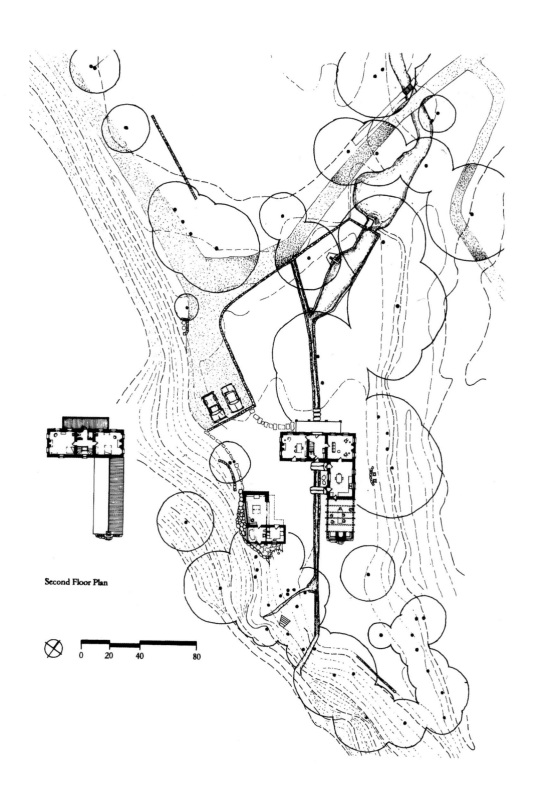

Second Floor Plan

0 20 40 80

Lyndhurst is the masterpiece of architect Alexander Jackson Davis, recognized as the preeminent designer of the residential Gothic Revival style. Asymmetrical in plan and irregular in outline, the house is built of a soft gray marble mottled with pale yellow that was quarried at nearby Ossining. Construction took place in two stages, the first occurring at the beginning of Gothic Revival's popularity and the other at its end.

The original house, known as Knoll for its hilltop site overlooking the Hudson River, was less imposing in size and name. Historian William H. Pierson Jr. described the house as "designed and oriented in relation to a particular and highly romantic natural setting. It was an experience in light, shadow, atmosphere, and texture; it was filled with contrasts and surprise."[12] Built for General William Paulding, commander in the War of 1812 and later mayor of New York City, Knoll was a simpler central-gable villa in "the pointed style," but with crenellated parapets, handsome chimneys, and rich stone ornamentation.

In 1864, merchant and inventor George Merritt bought the house and the second phase of its development began. His social ambitions required a grander setting, so he set about almost doubling the house's size and changing its name to the more literary sounding Lyndhurst. Although by the time the house was completed American architecture had moved beyond Gothic Revival to other equally romantic styles, Davis designed what was a seamless addition in the original style, further enriching the house's irregularity with towers, turrets, and picturesque pinnacles.

The Gothic style afforded Davis the freedom that allowed Knoll to flow easily into Lyndhurst. Without destroying his original creation, Davis achieved an uninterrupted transformation and an organic continuity. Lyndhurst is often mentioned in company with Jefferson's Monticello, both houses celebrated for their intelligent and provocative designs.

A corner of the veranda that wraps around the house.

Lyndhurst, originally known as Knoll,
was built on a hilltop overlooking the
Hudson River in Tarrytown, New York.
Design and construction took place
in two stages, 1838 and 1865, both
executed by Alexander Jackson Davis.
The soft gray marble of the exterior
was quarried at nearby Ossining.

ABOVE: The original house was a simpler central-gable villa, but with crenellated parapets and handsome chimneys. The section on the right in this photograph is part of the second phase of development. The lower-floor windows of the newer section are wider than those of the original house. Nevertheless, the architect's command of the Gothic Revival style allowed Knoll to flow seamlessly into Lyndhurst.

OPPOSITE: Davis created the opulent dining room as part of the 1865 addition. The pointed Gothic arches surrounding the room are its dominant feature. They are supported on fluted columns; the two flanking the fireplace are of marble, and the others are of painted wood. The chairs are also of Davis's design.

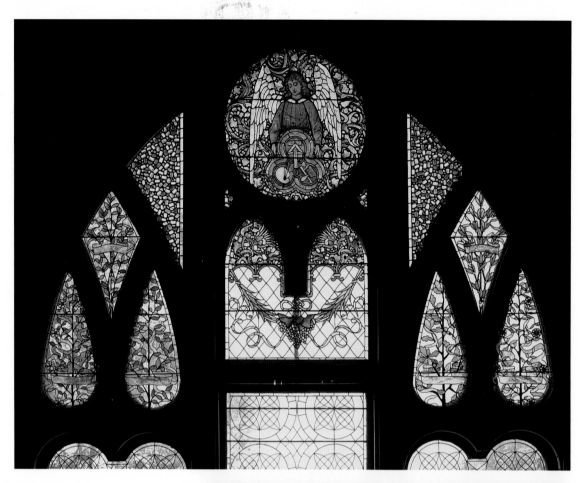

OPPOSITE: This stately bedroom extends over the original porte cochère. The bed, its headboard and finials echoing the pointed window's tracery, is a remarkable example of Gothic Revival furniture.

LEFT: A spectacular Gothic window overlooking the Hudson River dominates what was originally the library. Replaced later in the nineteenth century, the magnificent stained glass is attributed to Louis Comfort Tiffany. It depicts an "Emblem of the Arts," with an angel holding a painter's palette, a sculptor's tools, and an architect's drafting set.

The library was converted to a picture gallery when the house was expanded in 1865. Its vaulted ceiling has exposed timbers with trefoil patterning. Davis designed the Gothic chairs in front of the window.

ABOVE: A light-filled bay in the parlor.

OPPOSITE: A particularly romantic
bedroom with its starry ceiling.

Ebenezer Maxwell's mansion, a villa of fanciful eclecticism, was completed in 1859. It was built of local Wissahickon schist and red sandstone, held together with mortar that was enhanced with coal dust to darken it and quartz sand to echo the flecks of mica in the schist. Neither Italianate nor Elizabethan, the house displays elements of both. The date of completion coincides with the popularity of the Italianate style, of which its campanile is a characteristic hallmark. At the same time, the stonework and gable patterns suggest Elizabethan England. It is reasonable to call this picturesque amalgam of elements simply Victorian.

Located in Germantown, then a rapidly developing suburb of Philadelphia, the architecture has not been attributed to a known architect, although it has been credited to Joseph C. Hoxie of Philadelphia, an acquaintance of Maxwell's. However, the floor plan is identical to a nearby earlier house designed by Samuel Sloan, also a friend of the owner.

Maxwell, a cloth merchant, was prosperous but not wealthy. His house, built as a speculative venture, incorporated the luxury of the latest modern conveniences, such as gas lighting, hot-air central heating, and indoor plumbing. He furnished it with sets of new mass-produced furniture rather than with the elaborate handmade pieces that might have been chosen by a wealthier man.

The villa is the only Victorian house museum in Philadelphia, a city where the events and architecture of the preceding century are emphasized. It is not the site of a notable event, nor the home of a famous citizen. Rather, it shows the life of a merchant's family during the time of the Industrial Revolution, when mass production replaced individual craftsmanship but also offered modern luxuries that eased living.

LEFT: The door in the sitting room adjoining one of the bedrooms has its original stenciling.

OPPOSITE: Built of the local Wissahickon schist and red sandstone, the Ebenezer Maxwell Mansion combines a number of architectural styles. The early mansard roof is intersected with Elizabethan gables, but the campanile is an Italianate element.

LEFT: With its mix of elements and fanciful stonework, the house is best termed simply Victorian.

BELOW: The living room is furnished with machine-made Rococo Revival pieces. The interior reflects a time when individual craftsmanship was superceded by mass production.

OPPOSITE: The stenciling and hand-painted designs in the stairwell are characteristic of the Aesthetic Movement.

Louis A. Benoist was a successful St. Louis banker who at his death in 1867 was one of the richest men in the nation. In 1850 he began assembling 485 acres of rolling land, which became Oakland Farm. Two years later he commissioned George I. Barnett to build an Italianate villa on the farm. Barnett, then possibly St. Louis's most famous architect, had built several fine Italianate houses for the city's wealthy during the 1840 and 1850s. Of those few houses remaining, Oakland, built of limestone quarried on the estate, is the best preserved and least changed structurally.

The Italianate style emerged about 1845, eventually supplanting the Gothic Revival as the dominant style for country houses. A key characteristic of Italian villas, the campanile tower is Oakland's most dramatic feature. A classical triangular pediment crowns the front-facing gable, and modillions support the roof's broad eaves. Such classical references evoked a level of grandeur that the elitist and literary Gothic Revival did not. More formal and less intricate than Gothic, the Italian Renaissance detailing gave a feeling of dignity and sophistication. At the same time, the asymmetrical, informal composition with loggias and wide verandas provided a sense of the picturesque. Houses in this style appealed to the rising class of wealthy citizens who represented the driving ambition of industrial America.

Oakland passed through several owners until 1977 when the Affton Historical Society acquired the then-dilapidated mansion and restored it to its original splendor. More than a museum, the house has become a community center, open to the public and available for various private events.

LEFT: Plaster cove moldings border fourteen-foot ceilings in one of the mansion's bedrooms.

OPPOSITE: Oakland was designed by George I. Barnett, possibly St. Louis's most famous architect, who built several Italianate mansions for wealthy St. Louisans in the 1840s and 1850s. It was constructed of limestone quarried on the estate.

Throughout the 1870s Henry Hobson Richardson built magnificent stone structures, tending toward increasingly sculptural expression based on the weight and textures of the material. In 1880, this evolution culminated in the rubble stonework of the Ames Gate Lodge, which, as historian Vincent Scully has said, "brought violently to the attention of American architects the expressive possibilities inherent in construction with rough stone, up to boulder size."[13]

Richardson looked to the land for inspiration in his residential designs, experimenting with geologic imagery. He used piled boulders and stones to create natural building forms. According to Henry-Russell Hitchcock, Richardson "seemed to be seeking his inspiration back in the time before architecture took form."[14] Scully comments, "In a poetic sense the Ames Gate Lodge represents an investigation into the primitive nature of a material. It is thus also concerned in the search for archetypes characteristic of its period."[15] By grounding his architectural vocabulary in the abstract, elemental forms of stone, Richardson created a thoroughly novel mode of expression.

OPPOSITE: The Ames Gate Lodge in North Easton, Massachusetts, is surrounded by grounds designed by Frederick Law Olmsted.

ABOVE: Richardson used piled boulders and stones to create expressive, natural building forms.

Richardson's trademark masonry arch
was much imitated in stone, brick, and
even wood by other architects.

An inglenook with a fireplace in the
Ames Gate Lodge.

Upon reviewing their house's final interior changes with client's John and Frances Glessner, Henry Hobson Richardson said, "There, Mr. Glessner, if I were to live five years longer, that is the last thing I would do to your house: my part is finished." Three weeks later, in 1886, Richardson, the greatest figure in American architecture in the 1870s and 1880s, was dead of Bright's disease at age forty-seven.[16]

When the Glessners first approached Richardson, he was scheduled to go to Chicago to design what would become one of the country's most noted buildings, the Marshall Field and Company block-square, wholesale store and warehouse. Fearing that he only designed public buildings, the Glessners were delighted with his reply to their hesitant inquiry. "I'll plan anything a man wants," he wrote, "from a cathedral to a chicken coop. That's the way I make my living."[17]

Richardson, whose reputation as America's most original architect was challenged only in the following century by Frank Lloyd Wright, created for the Glessners a house of great distinction and urban monumentality, if also one of considerable controversy. Unlike neighboring houses with their walls of smoothly finished ashlar stonework, the Glessner House is faced in courses of massive, rough-faced stone, which itself serves as the decorative element. The cutting and laying of the stone created an organizational pattern, giving the house visual strength and unity. Three belt courses of slightly more finished stone subtly mark the three floors, one running above the entrance door, the second below the first-floor windows, and the third topping the third-floor windows.

As severe and simple as the street facades are, the interior courtyard gives way to a more decorative treatment. The walls are brick with windows trimmed in the same pale granite of the street facade and topped with conical towers not unlike those of the neighboring buildings.

In order to preserve the house as Richardson had designed it, the Glessners continued to live in it long after the neighborhood ceased to be fashionable. In 1924, Mr. Glessner donated the house to the American Institute of Architects, which in the Depression could not afford to preserve it. The house went through a series of owners until 1966 when a foundation was formed to acquire it and preserve it as it is today, a house museum open to the public.

OPPOSITE LEFT: Richardson's signature Romanesque-inspired details, such as the round arch with articulated voussoirs, the carved tympanum, and the engaged columns with carved capitals, appear at the entrance bay.

OPPOSITE RIGHT: The interior courtyard has brick walls trimmed in pale granite, creating a softer, less formal look than that of the street facade.

RIGHT: The imposing rusticated stone facade of the Glessner House dominates the streetscape.

Richardson modeled the Glessners'
library, with its massive desk and
beamed ceiling, after his own.

The living hall, with its welcoming fireplace, warm wood paneling, and broad staircase, is the spatial core of the house rather than just a circulation area. Richardson's transformation of this space in his interior planning was an innovation in American architecture.

STIMSON RESIDENCE

CARROLL H. BROWN   EXPOSITION PARK   LOS ANGELES, CALIFORNIA   1891

Romanesque Revival—or Richardsonian Romanesque—began with the architect's designs in the 1870s, was adopted in the 1880s by those who could afford houses in the style, reached its height of popularity in city row houses in the 1890s after Richardson's death, and fell out of favor by 1900. Intended for large, freestanding houses and public buildings, the style lost something of its finesse in hands other than Richardson's. City rowhouses and spec houses generally featured a tower, an arch, or a rusticated column to qualify as Romanseque Revival.

The Stimson house, designed by Carroll H. Brown for an early Chicago lumber tycoon, is a mansion of rough-cut red sandstone, the material synonymous with town houses of the era. Of the few Romanesque Revival residences in Los Angeles, it is considered to be the best. In an exuberant use of Romanesque features, the house combines many, if not all, of the style's characteristic elements: a four-story octagonal tower, a recessed arched porch on the third floor, corbeled eaves, round-topped windows, a deeply recessed entrance porch with an arched door flanked by columns, more columns and colonnettes (single and grouped), a bay window, and carved decoration of stylized foliage. Although recessed in keeping with the style, the one-over-one double-hung sash windows were very much the vogue in a "modern" house such as this one.

Surrounded by semitropical landscaping, this high-style dwelling calls attention to the difference between California's climate and that of Richardson's northern clime. It may better be called California Romanesque.

One of the few surviving Romanesque Revival residences in the Los Angeles area, the Stimson house, with its exuberant use of historical elements and semi-tropical landscaping, might well be called California Romanesque.

Tuxedo Park, created by tobacco magnate Pierre Lorillard more than one hundred years ago as a sportsman's preserve, is thirty-eight miles and about an hour from New York City in the foothills of the Ramapo Mountains. In 1886, Lorillard commissioned Bruce Price to develop the twenty-five hundred parklike acres with roads, a village, stables, and a clubhouse, plus twenty-two new houses. Price's early designs in Tuxedo Park were Shingle Style cottages, a mode he brought to such perfection that Frank Lloyd Wright borrowed heavily from the details of one example for his own house in Oak Park, Illinois. But by the 1890s wood-shingled cottages were not grand enough for the new breed of wealthy, cosmopolitan Americans who became covetous of the aristocratic Old World mansions they saw on their transatlantic voyages.

Boulder Point is a magnificent rough-stone example of the type of monumental construction that Price and other leading architects built in revival styles—Gothic, Jacobean, Tudor, Queen Anne—during the 1890s to meet the demands of clients with new fortunes. From its terra-cotta-tiled and gabled roof to its superb stonework, the house exhibits workmanship of that bygone era. Overlooking Tuxedo Lake with twelve hundred feet of shoreline, the house has water views from virtually each of the twenty-four rooms. Stone terraces link the indoors with the surrounding natural beauty outside.

Tuxedo Park has gone through times of great fortunes and times of their loss. During the Depression, many mansions were demolished or burned down; others simply decayed. In the 1950s and 1960s, new residents were attracted to the smaller, more manageable outbuildings—the potting sheds, stables, and carriage houses—which they renovated, adding to Tuxedo's charm. With the prosperity of the 1990s, many of the great mansions have been restored. Few communities can boast so many architecturally significant houses in excellent condition. Fortunately, Boulder Point is owned by a couple experienced in historic preservation. They have painstakingly removed inappropriate alterations and restored the house to its original design.

OPPOSITE AND ABOVE: Boulder Point, designed by Bruce Price in 1890, is a magnificent rough-stone example of his work for elite clients in the exclusive residential community of Tuxedo Park. It overlooks Tuxedo Lake with twelve hundred feet of shoreline and has water views from most of its twenty-four rooms.

LEFT: The paneled dining room at Boulder Point has seating for sixteen.

The sun porch retains its original stone walls and floor. The present owners have carefully restored and refurbished Boulder Point to Bruce Price's original design.

Biltmore, a 225-room mansion in the style of the French Renaissance, was created for George W. Vanderbilt by the nation's most prominent architect, Richard Morris Hunt (1827–1895), and the equally renowned landscape architect, Frederick Law Olmsted (1822–1903). The palatial, Indiana limestone mansion was the largest and most celebrated residence of its time, a monument to its owner's personal vision of aristocratic country life, farfetched perhaps, but nevertheless his dream.

George Vanderbilt and his brother Frederick, whose house on the Hudson River is also featured in this book (see pages 118–21), were third-generation members of one of America's richest families. George was the youngest of the eight children of William Henry Vanderbilt, who, in turn, was the eldest son and principal heir of Commodore Cornelius Vanderbilt, founder of the family fortune. Bookish and introspective, George, a twenty-six-year-old bachelor, chose to concentrate a large part of his $10 million inheritance on the construction of Biltmore and the development of its estate, originally some 125,000 acres of of land in Asheville, North Carolina.

Vanderbilt had at first considered a simpler style for his country house. But his Ecole des Beaux-Arts–trained architect, Hunt, favored French architecture. His Chateauesque designs had already become the rage among monied Americans. Hunt convinced Vanderbilt to visit the châteaux of the Loire Valley before making a decision.

Biltmore was the largest and most successful example of Hunt's residential work. He drew on the forms of such renowned châteaux as Chambord, Blois, and Chenonceaux, combining their spires, turrets, and steep slate roofs into a work as original as it was lavish. More than a historical pastiche, however, the house shows Hunt's genius for integrating the architecture of the past in a strong composition adapted to contemporary needs. Situated among gardens, parks, lakes, and woodlands, the house belonged to the site as much as it took advantage of it. Tragically, Hunt died a few months before the house was opened.

Like another genius architect of the time, Henry Hobson Richardson, Hunt created his own very personal interpretation of a style, freely adapting historical precedents to create the Chateauesque. Short-lived, it was limited in influence due to its high-style aspirations and its expensive stonework.

LEFT: For Biltmore, Richard Morris Hunt drew on forms of the great châteaux of France—Chambord, Blois, and Chenonceaux—combining spires, turrets, and steep slate roofs into a work that was as original as it was opulent.

OPPOSITE: Biltmore was originally surrounded by 125,000 acres. The estate was the greatest achievement of two of the most renowned designers in the country: Richard Morris Hunt, its architect, and Frederick Law Olmsted, its landscape architect.

VANDERBILT MANSION   MᴄKIM, MEAD & WHITE   HYDE PARK, NEW YORK   1896–99

In domestic architecture, the Beaux-Arts style (also known as American Renaissance) belonged to the wealthy elite. Unlike almost all other American design modes, which filtered down from high-style residences to the more modest dwellings of the average homeowner, Beaux-Arts remained the province of those who could afford monuments to opulence. Almost always constructed of pale ashlar limestone or marble and encrusted with ornament, such mansions were rooted in the classicism of ancient Greece and Rome as well as the Italian Renaissance. The style was elaborated with details such as paired Corinthian columns, friezes, garlands, and sculpture.

McKim, Mead & White designed this Beaux-Arts country house for Frederick W. Vanderbilt and his wife, Louise. Sited at Hyde Park with an expansive view of the Hudson River, and surrounded by a picturesque park, the house was tastefully elegant. Although sufficiently grand with its splendid entrance, its entablature crowned by a massive sculpture, and its Corinthian porticoes, it was restrained compared to the edifices of Vanderbilt's better-known kin, such as the Breakers and Marble House in Newport. Although the house was built for aristocratic life, it was not the intention of this branch of the family to exhibit such grandiose palatial taste. However, as Mark Alan Hewitt observes of these Vanderbilts, "That their house ended up looking as it did gives credence to the assumption that at certain levels of society in the 1890s it was impossible to avoid a regal life."[18]

Beaux-Arts architecture became popular for many public buildings, such as libraries, banks, and courthouses. In domestic design, the Vanderbilt Mansion is among the finest examples of the style. It is now a National Historic Site.

LEFT: George A. Glaenzer of New York City decorated the library, used by the Vanderbilts as a family living room.

OPPOSITE: The Beaux-Arts residence of Indiana limestone was elaborately designed. Symmetrically paired Corinthian columns support the porticoes, and the facade is adorned with sumptuous floral friezes, lions' heads, and an elaborate entablature above the entrance.

OPPOSITE: The grand staircase has an intricate wrought-iron banister.

ABOVE: Stanford White acquired the dining room's seventeenth-century coffered ceiling and the Renaissance mantel on a European buying trip.

Chestnut Hill, one of Philadelphia's suburbs, was a farming community in colonial times. Change began when the first rail line from downtown Philadelphia opened in 1854 and the community was incorporated into the city. Chestnut Hill and the many other charming rural areas surrounding the city grew into residential enclaves as city folk sought relief from the increasing stresses of industrial urban life.

Beginning in 1880 Henry Howard Houston and, later, his son-in-law, Dr. George Woodward, acquired large tracts of land and developed the dominant residential fabric of much of Chestnut Hill. Dr. Woodward and his wife, Gertrude, Houston's daughter, continued the rental housing begun by her father, creating a series of influential housing complexes of which the French Village subdivision, designed by Robert R. McGoodwin, was one.

From 1880 to the Depression wealthy families built country retreats throughout the area, ranging from large estates to substantial houses along Germantown Avenue and other village streets. Through the architecture of their homes the city's conservative citizens sought to identify with their ancestors. Thus, the romantic appeal of the Anglo-French pastoral style produced many houses of rustic character. In addition, the period saw houses built in other popular revival styles.

The Wissahickon schist of Philadelphia and the Delaware Valley had supplied stone for the area's vernacular architecture dating back as far as the seventeenth century. It is everywhere evident in Chestnut Hill's later suburban development, a perfect match for these European-influenced styles and the skills of the area's Italian masons.

OPPOSITE: The picturesque tower corner of a Chestnut Hill house.

RIGHT: A Gate's Lane house in the French Village subdivision, which was designed by Robert R. McGoodwin. The common use of the local stone gives Chestnut Hill its particular character and continuity.

Architect Walter H. Thomas designed
this French-influenced house in 1917.
The stonework is particularly fine.

ABOVE: A house in the French Village section recalls the pastoral architecture of France.

LEFT: A Tudor Revival Cotswold-style house in Chestnut Hill.

A charming house in the French Village, complete with wooden shutters and a garden wall.

ABOVE: A house in the Cotswold Court section of Chestnut Hill.

This unusual Queen Anne house, designed by the architectural firm of Cope & Stewardson in 1890, has many of the elements that characterize the style. The steeply pitched roof is intersected with equally steep gables. An oriel with small windowpanes, a conically roofed tower, and a wraparound veranda (not shown) are all elements of the Queen Anne mode, which became popular in the United States following the Centennial Exhibition of 1876 in Philadelphia.

The style derives from a contemporaneous English fashion based on early eighteenth-century manor houses. In America the style incorporated Colonial Revival details and was among the more eclectic of the many Victorian styles, taking form in a variety of materials, including brick, clapboard, and shingle. This Chestnut Hill house was built of the area's ubiquitous stone.

Cope & Stewardson, the designers of this unusual Queen Anne style house built in 1890, were among the many prominent architects designing in Chestnut Hill in the late nineteenth century. An addition was done by architects Brockie & Hastings in 1909.

COLONIAL REVIVAL HOUSE   MANTLE FIELDING   CHESTNUT HILL, PENNSYLVANIA   1895

Following Philadelphia's 1876 Centennial Exhibition, which generated society's pride in the country and its origins, the Georgian and Federal styles became newly popular. Freely drawn from their precedents, these revival styles tend to be merely reminiscent of the architecture of the colonial period and the early years of the republic, and they are often referred to generally as Colonial Revival.

Designed by the Philadelphia architect Mantle Fielding, this house is an early example of the Georgian Revival. The symmetrical facade is bowed on each side of the entrance, which is fronted by a deep porch. The gabled roof has multiple dormers, and the windows flanking the entrance are embellished with broken pediments, a borrowed eighteenth-century detail that most obviously identifies the house's precedent.

However, paired and grouped windows never appeared in Georgian and Federal houses; therefore, the window treatment immediately gives away the age of the house. Liberties were often taken with proportion and scale in the Colonial Revival, as seen in the massive quality created by the stonework.

This Colonial Revival–style house is executed in "Chestnut Hill stone," the Wissahickon mica schist common to the area.

To give his house an indigenous quality, Charles Lummis faced the front exterior and bell tower with boulders taken from the Arroyo Seco. The house is stuccoed at the rear.

EL ALISAL, CHARLES F. LUMMIS HOUSE HIGHLAND PARK, CALIFORNIA CIRCA 1895
AND
ARROYO SECO ROCK HOUSES PASADENA, CALIFORNIA

At the high end of the materials spectrum, stone is a status material because of its implied expense. Quarrying, transporting, cutting, and laying take time and money. However, stone is also a material at the low end of the spectrum, a material free for the taking from fields, shores, and canyon washes by anyone willing to haul it away.

At the turn of the twentieth century and into its early decades the Arroyo Seco, a canyon running through Pasadena, Highland Park, and into Los Angeles, furnished house builders with water-rounded granite stones—beautiful, bountiful, and available at no expense. Like upstate New York with its cobblestone houses, Southern California developed a folk tradition of vernacular stone dwellings. This development coincided with the arrival of Portland cement mortar as well as with the Arts and Crafts movement and the popular enthusiasm for nature and natural materials.

Charles F. Lummis, author, historian, and archeologist—among his many accomplishments and interests—designed this Mission Revival house and built it largely with his own hands over a fifteen-year period. With the help of Isleta Indians, he dragged boulders from the nearby arroyo and masoned them into the facade of his castle. (It was simply stuccoed on the rear.) The interior was fashioned as a rustic cabin. Much of the wood- and metalwork was handcrafted by Lummis or by artist friends. One of the best-known of the boulder houses, El Alisal, as Lummis named it, is open to the public.

In nearby Tujunga Canyon the stones differ from those of the Arroyo Seco. They are more jagged, giving the buildings a different effect. Many do-it-yourself houses were built there from the 1890s to the 1920s.

The Long Beach earthquake of 1933 took its toll on these rock houses and effectively put an end to this vernacular stone tradition. The very structures that looked so durable were particularly vulnerable to earthquakes. Even so, many such houses have survived a century of earthquakes, as well as freeway extensions.

The Craftsman ethic of handicrafts was carried through in the detailing of the Lummis House interiors, which were decorated with Native American baskets, rugs, and pottery.

The living room incorporated contemporary Arts and Crafts designs.

Furniture, such as this cupboard in the dining room, was handcrafted by Lummis himself or by artist friends.

OPPOSITE: The mission-inspired gable with its bell reflects Lummis's interest in the area's Spanish-Mexican past.

An Arroyo Seco house using both round and split boulders. It has the low-pitched roof and rafter ends associated with the Arts and Crafts bungalow style.

LEFT: An imaginative Arroyo Seco design, this house combines Arts and Crafts elements and perhaps some Swiss chalet details in its boulder construction.

CHAPTER 4

TWENTIETH CENTURY

Much of the twentieth century was marked by strongly contrasting stylistic currents in the design of houses. While industry was forging the way to a more complex future, people were also casting nostalgic backward glances to a simpler time. While the avant-garde was dedicated to establishing a new industrial aesthetic, a traditional trend produced the full flowering of historicism.[1]

This architectural dichotomy began about 1885. The years between then and 1915 were turbulent times for American society. With the influx of foreign immigrants, the population was exploding. The industrial economy was rapidly expanding, giving people more jobs and more money. Ingenious inventions were multiplying. Such developments as the telephone and the incandescent lightbulb would help literally to light the way to new lifestyles. Thanks to the commuter railroad, later followed by the private automobile, a revolution in transportation was underway. After 1885, as the pace of cultural change grew, architects felt the need for a clearer sense of order, consolidation, and controlling discipline in their work, as well as an architecture that would better adapt to modern living patterns. In their quest many turned to the security of historical associations and classical forms hoping to find the new by adapting the old to new uses and requirements. This trend in American architecture abandoned the picturesque of the Victorian years and returned to the kind of formal order and symmetry that had gone out about 1850 with Greek Revival. It was in this climate that Chicago's 1893 World's Columbian Exposition appeared, as Leland Roth says, "like a dream."

The architects appointed by Daniel Burnham to design the various buildings of the fair agreed early on that unity of expression was a requirement. To achieve it, of necessity the classical style would be used since it was the only one they all knew equally well. The harmony of the classical and Renaissance forms of the fair's pristine white buildings set against Chicago's gritty industrial backdrop was greeted by the public with great enthusiasm. The fair would have a profound effect on architecture of the day.[2]

The influential Ecole des Beaux-Arts in Paris, bastion of nineteenth-century classicism, was a training ground for many American architects. Beaux-Arts principles emphasized axial formality and balance. Smooth ashlar stonework replaced rough rubble, and glittering white limestone villas, grandiose granite palazzi, or marble mansions superceded the polychrome stone buildings that were previously fashionable. The grandeur of Beaux-Arts classical forms appealed to the wealthy of the Gilded Age. Many residences were designed in the elaborate style, characterized by decorative stone columns, cartouches, swags, garlands, and statuary. Although the Beaux-Arts style faded in the dark days of the Great Depression, classical principles remained entrenched in American architecture, if in a less flamboyant form.

While the Columbian Exposition gave rise to a return to classical design, it also awakened an interest in America's colonial past. As a result, Colonial Revival, a style that borrowed heavily

PREVIOUS SPREAD: The living room of the Hooper house in Baltimore, Maryland, designed by Marcel Breuer and his associate Herbert Beckhard in 1960.

from early American Georgian and Federal designs—also rooted in classical orders—became the vogue. With the influential architectural firm of McKim, Mead & White leading the way in adapting these historical styles, many prestigious architects followed in designing large residences—much larger than the colonial originals—for well-heeled clients.

To Frank Lloyd Wright such revival and classical styles had little to do with the modern social patterns of the American family. Wright, too, was searching for a more ordered, integrated architecture, one that would better adapt to contemporary life. However, he went his own way, developing a quite different vocabulary of clean lines and free-flowing spaces. By 1900 Wright's aesthetic had evolved into the celebrated Prairie Style houses. An open floor plan with fewer separate rooms simplified living for families. Walls were replaced with sliding panels, a feature inspired by Japanese architecture, which Wright admired. The central living space established a dominant axis around which other rooms were grouped, and a stone hearth and chimney anchored the house to its site.

Low-lying on the flat Midwestern terrain, Wright's houses appeared to grow organically from their sites; by extending their horizontal planes with broad, overhanging roofs and spreading terraces they were integrated with the land. Wright achieved what many architects had been searching for, a truly national style. His Prairie houses were the first uniquely American residential architecture.

While Wright was working in Chicago, in California the Craftsman designs of brothers Charles and Henry Greene were also making an impact. Greene & Greene's houses, like many of Wright's, featured the simple beauty of natural, hand-worked materials—wood and stone—that helped to integrate house and site. An attempt to reintroduce a human approach to architecture and design and to resist the forces of industrialization gave rise to the allied Arts and Crafts movement and its use of stone, a material unsuited to machines, as well as hand-finished wood, wrought iron, and leaded and stained glass. Craftsman bungalows are characterized by extensive rubble stonework on ground floors, porches, and pillars. Like the work of the Prairie School, these Craftsman designs emphasized comfort and convenience, features that would continue to reverberate in the small-scale suburban house.

The search for order that had begun in the 1880s continued until World War I when residential construction stopped. When the war ended, society hoped to return to normal life, but that was not to be. The world had changed. The revolution in transportation that began in the nineteenth century had culminated in automobile production on a mass scale. By 1920, a Model T Ford was rolling off the production line every twenty seconds. The private automobile permanently altered American life and American architecture. Society gained rural mobility, which would in time see farmland transformed into country estates and suburban developments. The

desire to escape the teeming, industrialized cities produced a great flight to the countryside led first by the upper class but soon followed by the middle class. If the source of their money was the city, the country was where they escaped its crowds and industrial blight.

Suburban communities around major cities grew rapidly. New York's Tuxedo Park, Philadelphia's Chestnut Hill and Main Line, Cleveland's Shaker Heights, and Chicago's Lake Forest, among others, experienced their greatest period of growth between 1910 and 1940. During those years the suburban house was a major concern of the architectural profession. Although designed with great eclectic freedom as to historic period, these houses generally drew on Renaissance or medieval precedents, with Tudor preferred. This architectural expression first took hold in estates for industrial barons.[3] Stone, frequently the material of choice for manor houses, was appropriate to such styles, but it was labor intensive as well as costly to quarry and transport. And for all that, stone had an aura of wealth and taste, proclaiming the success of the houses' occupants.

Historicism was prevalent in the architecture of the growing suburbs. Anxiety caused by the rapidly changing culture created nostalgia for a time before the Industrial Revolution; it also allowed the country's new wealthy class to acquire status by identifying with the landed gentry of their European forebears. Tudor and Colonial Revival styles challenged each other for popularity. The Colonial style appealed to nostalgia for a younger America, while Tudor satisfied a yearning for English roots and, as Mark Alan Hewitt writes, "the flavor of antiquity." Tudor houses had the added "cachet of expensive materials—copper, slate, and especially stone." Thousands of Tudoresque houses, with half-timbering, rustic stone, and a medieval quality, were built

OPPOSITE: Detail of a 1923 Tudor Revival house designed by Meade & Hamilton in Shaker Heights, Ohio.

RIGHT: Detail of the entrance to Windswept, a 1928–31 mansion designed by David Adler in Lake Forest, Illinois.

first in exclusive country-club communities outside major cities, later filtering down to middle-class suburbs throughout the country.[4] Meanwhile, in contrast to these conservative modes, a completely different aesthetic had come to America: modernism.

The modernist movement rejected historical references and ornament. European architects Mies van der Rohe, Walter Gropius, Rudolph Schindler, Richard Neutra, and Marcel Breuer, coming to the United States in the 1920s and 1930s, imported with them the early modernist principles that would come to be known as the International Style. Accelerating industrial technology mechanized building techniques, giving rise to the modern villa with unadorned, crisp white walls and steel and all-glass facades. Building elements became standardized, prefabricated, and interchangeable. Technology freed walls from their conventional load-bearing function and allowed large expanses of glass. New materials suited to the machine were made available—poured concrete, plywood, steel framing, glass blocks, chrome.

The machine dominated during the 1920s, and stone, an incompatible material, seemed little suited to the modernist aesthetic. However, an interest in the vernacular developed concurrently. European modernist architects drew analogies between the simplicity of folk forms and those of the machine. Both were seen as an architectural expression of existing conditions of time and place. Between 1930 and 1935 Le Corbusier explored this notion, building three stone vacation villas, two on the Riviera and one in Chile, using local building techniques while nevertheless maintaining his modernist ideals.

These stone villas were to influence Marcel Breuer in his use of local stone. When he came to the United States, Breuer employed stone in several modernist houses, taking advantage of the material's geometry and precision of line in cubist massing, while its natural textures and colors were the perfect foil for clean, hard-edged forms. Unlike the machine-inspired designs of the International Style, which produced the house as a distinct object on the land, it was Breuer's use of stone that merged his strictly modernist houses with their landscape. Open planning and the combination of stone with glass and plywood successfully melded interior and exterior. His willingness to use local stone and local building techniques helped to introduce the new modernism to a broader population.[5]

Nevertheless, mainstream America preferred traditional dwellings built with traditional materials. Many found sterile the abstract expressions in concrete, glass, and steel. As a result, when building resumed after World War II, architects and their more conventional clients rejected this architecture that generally failed to consider site, climate, and local materials.

Architects began to employ alternative designs and approaches in order to expand the modernist idiom. In the mid-1960s, the rise of the preservation movement led to a revival of interest in the American vernacular. Without completely discarding the principles of modernism, architects again considered the relationship of the building to its environment as well as folk solutions to problems such as climate and landscape. Through the use of materials such as stone and wood they designed structures to reflect the natural setting, joining house with landscape by bringing indoors the natural materials of the surroundings.

In the 1980s postmodernism, rejecting modernism's severity and orthodoxy, promoted a broader interplay of materials and the reintroduction of ornament. The movement's wider use of sources of inspiration for design included landscape, color, and natural materials. If Mies van der Rohe proclaimed, "Less is more," postmodernism famously replied, "Less is a bore." Postmodernism deliberately referred to the past, using playful geometries, ornament, and surface detailing in reaction to modernism's unadorned boxes that seemed to disregard their context. In its purest form, postmodernism made jocular use of the classical vocabulary, overblowing or distorting a pediment, for example, and using it as applied ornament.

The exuberant economic period of the 1980s and 1990s created more wealth for people to spend on their residences. It led to what one architect called a golden age of building, one that included increased use of stone. In some cases people chose stone for its implied status of wealth. However, many architects contend that clients simply wanted to build in stone in protest against the shoddy and impermanent building practices of the time. Rather, they sought the permanence, solidity, and authenticity that stone offers.

The dichotomy between the avant-garde and tradition continued. With building parcels becoming scarce, many architects participated in knocking down existing houses in order to replace them with much larger ones that were often simply restatements of the Shingle Style or other period revival styles, overblown look-alike dwellings that came to be referred to as McMansions. Other architects remained committed to the modernist ethic of the house as an object on the land, further experimenting with the arrangement of forms in space. Architecture at its best in the 1990s was practiced by those striving to create their own unique contemporary designs, often drawing inspiration from vernacular sources and local materials such as stone for reinterpretation in the modern idiom. At the end of the century, American residential architecture continued to be as marked by contrasting stylistic currents as it had been at the beginning of the century.

In 1913, James Deering, a bachelor and the scion of a farm-machinery family, chose to build his extraordinary winter house in Miami, then a remote wilderness. When he retired as vice-president of Chicago's International Harvester Company, he was fifty-one years old.

Deering hired New York designer Paul Chalfin, who had extensive fine-arts credentials, to help him plan his house. The imperious Chalfin handled all of the house's details, including the hiring of an architect, Beaux-Arts–trained F. Burrall Hoffman Jr. (1882–1980). Extravagant buying trips to Italy yielded artifacts and parts of Renaissance villas; Vizcaya had to be of a scale worthy of the acquisitions. And so the project grew. Its design emphasized the antique architectural elements and furnishings and reflected several periods in the European decorative arts, beginning with the early Renaissance and ending with Neoclassicism.

The exterior and gardens of Vizcaya are in the style of the late Italian Renaissance. Two of the main themes of Italian gardens, water and architectural stonework, can be seen in the property's fountains and walls. The stone, exterior and interior, is from quarries in Cuba and Miami. Much of it is coquina stone, a coarse, porous limestone composed of shells and loosely cemented by calcite. An indigenous Florida stone, coquina was used extensively by Spanish settlers in Florida.

Chalfin and Hoffman gave Deering an astonishing seventy-room palazzo, something beyond anything Deering, who professed originally to want only a simple country house, could possibly have envisioned. He was able to luxuriate in his house only a few years, dying in 1926 while on an ocean crossing.

The gardens are considerably reduced from their original size. Deering's heirs, hard-pressed to maintain the estate, were forced to sell 130 of its 180 acres in 1945. In 1952, the county Parks and Recreation Department finally agreed to purchase the estate at a low price. The heirs donated the house's furnishings only after they were convinced the house was being well managed as a house museum.[6]

Paul Chalfin, a New York interior designer, directed the overall design of Vizcaya and its contents.

OPPOSITE: Vizcaya, an extraordinary palazzo in the style of the Italian Renaissance, incorporates details and fragments acquired from authentic Italian villas. The gardens were designed by Diego Suarez, a graduate of the Accademia dei Belle Arti in Florence.

ABOVE: An arcade borders the interior courtyard, which was conceived to promote cross ventilation through the house.

RIGHT: Vizcaya occupies a glorious site on Biscayne Bay.

To differentiate between where the cliff ends and the house begins is almost impossible. And that was architect Charles Greene's intention. The house appears to be a natural outcropping of the cliff. A boulder at the base of a wall belongs to the cliff, but above it eroded granite stones of Greene's careful choosing form the first few courses of the wall, with smaller ones climbing and melding into the house.

Charles Greene had never built a house completely of stone, although he and his brother Henry of the celebrated Greene & Greene partnership had used stonework in combination with other materials in the Arts and Crafts tradition. After retiring from the partnership, Charles moved to Carmel for a quieter life. Not long after, he received the commission to design this summer retreat for D. L. James, a prosperous merchant of china and glass from Kansas City, Missouri. The site is a rectangular granite promontory that sits a spectacular eighty feet above the ocean along the rugged coastline. Curving the house around the promontory formed a courtyard, which sheltered the occupants from the sometimes hurricane-force ocean winds.

It is a tribute to James that he put up with Greene's obsessive insistence on perfection. The architect, who was on site daily, oversaw the laying of individual stones. Charles Miller wrote, "It is the texture of the stonework that puts the James house into a league of its own among stone buildings, and its assembly was an exercise in tenacity." The clay tiles of the roof, for example, are "arranged in lines that curve and wiggle as they move up the roof, enhancing the organic colors and lines."[7]

The project had begun in 1918. By 1920, James realized what a passion the house had become for Greene, one that might never end. Nevertheless, he tolerated the architect's process until finally, after five years of construction, the ever-patient owner decided that enough was more than enough, and it was time for him to enjoy his house before he was driven to financial ruin. His forbearance paid off for both owner and architect. The house that Charles Greene created for D. L. James was a masterpiece.

LEFT: A resting place to enjoy the aroma of sea air mixed with eucalyptus and jasmine.

OPPOSITE: Sited on a promontory eighty feet above the sea, the house grips the side of the cliff like a giant hand, its foundations melded into the crevices so that boulders of the house and those of the cliff are indistinguishable. The house appears to rise as a formation of the cliff.

ABOVE: The living room, which is oriented to take advantage of the views.

OPPOSITE: The entrance courtyard, which shelters occupants from Carmel's sometimes gale-force winter winds.

Charles Greene, working with the
masons, supervised the laying of individual stones. He employed various
forms of arches and built deep reveals
around the windows.

The view from the library window.

OPPOSITE: The tower rises above the courtyard arcade. Greene's architecture was based on using natural materials to their best advantage, in keeping with the Arts and Crafts ethic. The golden-hued stone he found in Carmel was a perfect medium.

LEFT: The north window of the living room.

The sunroom library, seen through a trio of arches, is opposite the entry, allowing the visitor an immediate glimpse of the ocean. The library's limestone coving meets the ceiling with intentional irregularities.

The front of Tor House and its garden. Robinson Jeffers built the structure with stones hauled from the beach below.

BELOW: A narrow window in the dining room frames a spectacular view.

OVERLEAF: Hawk Tower and Tor House are joined by a courtyard and gardens.

By the time the poet Robinson Jeffers came to Carmel in the second decade of the twentieth century most artifacts of the Spanish Mission style that had been the village's early architectural heritage had been fragmented, compromised, or demolished. A new vernacular architecture developed as the community attracted writers and artists, thanks to the dream of two San Franciscans, Frank Deverdorf and Frank Powers, who in 1900 purchased most of the available land. Although displaying great range and variety, the vernacular cottages each seem dedicated to honoring nature and preserving a sense of this special place on the rugged coastline.

For his own house, Jeffers was influenced by the facades of barns he had seen in England. To duplicate them, he had granite boulders hauled from the beach below, using heavy ropes and horses. Jeffers then carefully chose each stone for the facade of Tor House, which he and M. J.

Murphy completed in 1919. Jeffers's wife, Una, was equally fascinated by the towers she had seen in England; at her urging, Jeffers added Hawk Tower in 1924.

The cottage is built close to the ground to minimize the effect of sharp winter winds coming off the ocean, while the tower, its top reached by a winding stair, takes in spectacular views of Carmel Bay and Pebble Beach. A writing space is provided on the ground floor. Using local materials, the house is in the vernacular tradition of cobblestone houses in other parts of the country. It also shows the Arts and Crafts movement's emphasis on the dignity of craftsmanship.

Tor House Foundation, established in 1978, oversees the property as a museum, preserving its architectural integrity and historic significance.[8]

OPPOSITE: A study in Hawk Tower.

LEFT: The ladies' retiring room in Hawk Tower.

The wood-paneled living room where Jeffers and his wife, Una, entertained guests.

Elizabethan, Jacobean, or Tudor, any house with half-timbering and a medieval cast could be referred to as Tudor in the years 1880 to 1940. Derived from sixteenth- and early-seventeenth-century English Renaissance architecture, Tudor Revival houses are rambling, asymmetrical mansions with steeply pitched roofs, intersecting gables, casement windows with leaded glass, and prominent chimneys. To homeowners, these Anglo-American styles were symbols of romance and roots, aristocracy and genteel living. First built by the wealthiest Americans, Tudor houses were soon in demand in the suburbs growing around major cities.

The Van Sweringen brothers, who developed the Cleveland suburb of Shaker Heights, exercised strict control over the development of the community. Prescribed house size depended on street and lot size. Recommended styles were Colonial, French, or English. In promotional material, the emphasis was on dignity and good taste. A competent architect was required to design the house, a rule that fortunately coincided with the careers of some of the country's outstanding architects working in the popular historic revivalist styles. Among them was the firm of Meade & Hamilton, who designed this early English Renaissance Tudor house in 1923.

Van Sweringen guidelines stressed distinctiveness of design and detail as well as integrity of architecture. The color of the sash had to be in harmony with the trim. Genuine lead bars were to be used in all glasswork instead of zinc, which was deemed flashy and "therefore not in good taste." With its fine stonework, this Tudor house clearly meets all the Van Sweringens' requirements.

ABOVE: Half-timbering, steep gables, elaborate chimneys, and window bays with leaded glass characterize the Tudor Revival, which was influenced by sixteenth- and seventeenth-century English architecture. In its heyday of the 1920s, the style was prevalent in suburban developments throughout the country.

OPPOSITE: A detail of the entrance and its fine stonework. The Tudor arch and diamond-paned casement windows are typical elements of the style.

Edwin Lundie is little known outside Minnesota, yet for those familiar with his work, he is one of the outstanding architects of the twentieth century. Born in 1886, he lived in a time when modernism was sweeping architecture. However, he rejected modernism as cold and sterile (as did many mainstream clients) and chose to remain true to his own style of picturesque romantic architecture. During his fifty-year career, he designed dwellings from simple cabins to large country estates, as well as public structures.

Dale Mulfinger, an architect who has written a book on Lundie,[9] says that he was a man of tradition, always referred to as "Mr. Lundie." He designed houses of careful detailing and proportion that showed his love of local materials, such as Minnesota's limestone.

This heavily rusticated limestone house is in a detailed Cotswold style with many gables and protruding eave lines. Situated on a bluff high above the Mississippi River, the house has a corner entry into a T plan with the circulation hub at the intersection of the bars of the T, allowing the projecting rooms to have light on three sides. Thanks to the skill of immigrant masons in using the local limestone, the house is in the regional vernacular tradition that first developed in the nineteenth century.

RIGHT: The entrance. Built of Minnesota limestone, the picturesque house shows architect Edwin Lundie's appreciation for local materials and fine craftsmanship.

OPPOSITE: The rear of the house, which has a T plan. Designed in the Cotswold style of intersecting gables, casement windows, and rusticated stone, it is a fine example of early-twentieth-century romantic architecture.

In 1924, Franklin Roosevelt had a fieldstone cottage built for his wife, Eleanor, on the Roosevelt estate overlooking the Hudson River in Dutchess County. Intended as a refuge from Springwood, the main house where her mother-in-law reigned, Val-Kil, Eleanor said, was the first house in her life that was truly hers.

Unlike the neoclassical Springwood, Val-Kil was in the vernacular Dutch style of the Hudson River valley. Two of Mrs. Roosevelt's friends lived in the cottage, and she spent time there whenever she was in Hyde Park.

Some years later, with Fascism on the rise and the economy in decline, Roosevelt decided that he, too, needed a refuge, a retreat to which he could escape from the pressures of his office. Among the many well-known facts about the president is that he was paralyzed by polio. It is less well known that he was one of only two sitting presidents to design a house for himself. The other, of course, was Thomas Jefferson.

In the late 1930s, Roosevelt began sending sketches to an architect friend, Henry J. Toombs, who had designed Val-Kil. Like Val-Kil, Top Cottage was in the Dutch vernacular style and built of local stone. The hilltop retreat that Roosevelt designed may be the first conceived by a disabled person for himself. Rather than steps to enter the house, an earthen ramp ran up to the porch on one side. Inside, the floors have no thresholds for a wheelchair to maneuver over, and windows are lower than usual. Wings off the central living room contain bedrooms and a kitchen. An open porch faces Hudson River sunsets. Roosevelt involved himself closely with details of the construction, particularly the stonework, which he wanted mortared to have wide joints.

The president never slept in the house, but visited it for times of relaxation with friends and, famously, entertained the king and queen of England there with a hot-dog cookout.

After Roosevelt's death, Top Cottage was sold twice, the owners making various changes. Finally, the Beaverkill Conservancy acquired it, restored it, and recently opened it to the public. Mrs. Roosevelt converted a defunct factory she had built next to Val-Kil, intended for the manufacture of reproductions of early American furniture, and it became her home. The stone cottage is used today by a group devoted to Eleanor Roosevelt's legacy.

Detail of Eleanor Roosevelt's Val-Kil cottage.

OPPOSITE: Val-Kil was designed in the vernacular Dutch Colonial style of the Hudson River Valley.

The east side of Val-Kil. Eleanor
Roosevelt often entertained friends
at her retreat.

Franklin Roosevelt's Top Cottage was his sanctuary from official public life. Roosevelt designed the house, also in the Dutch Colonial style, with his physical disability in mind. An earthen ramp once ran up to the side of the porch for wheelchair access.

David Adler (1882–1949) established himself as one of the Midwest's finest eclectic architects of the first half of the twentieth century, designing some fifty houses from the late 1910s to the 1930s in styles including Italian Renaissance, French Château, Georgian, and American Colonial. His practice was devoted to private houses and country clubs, much of it on Chicago's North Shore, although other important works exist in wealthy enclaves across the country.

Adler's Beaux-Arts training can be seen in this symmetrical, classically proportioned Georgian Revival masterpiece, constructed of gray Pennsylvania stone. Perfectly scaled—although much larger than any precedents from which it was adopted—it is a neoclassical villa comprising a central structure with two wings connecting to twin pavilions. The

wings, rather than mere passages, contain a pressing room and a flower room. Known as Windswept, the residence presides serenely on a high bluff, taking in its vast sweep of lakeshore vistas.

One of Adler's most outstanding designs, the house was built for Kersey Coates Reed and his wife, Helen, the daughter of John G. Shedd, president of Marshall Field & Co. Mrs. Reed was widowed during construction. (Later, she and her sister donated the original building of the Shedd Aquarium at the south end of Chicago's Grant Park.) Windswept is notable for its graceful interiors, which were executed by Frances Elkins, Adler's sister.[10] The present owners, Herbert F. and Dolores Stride, take great pride in preserving one of the masterpieces of Lake Forest.

ABOVE: Windswept, a symmetrical, classically proportioned Georgian Revival residence, is constructed of gray Pennsylvania stone. Its architect, David Adler, was one of the finest eclectic architects of the first half of the twentieth century, designing many houses for clients on Chicago's North Shore as well as in other wealthy enclaves across the country.

OPPOSITE: Adler was renowned for his staircases. Belgian marble columns flank this graceful staircase, which has an ebony banister and wrought-glass spindles.

OPPOSITE: The Beaux-Arts–trained Adler borrowed from classical precedents and was noted for his attention to detail.

LEFT: The entrance hall, looking into the living room.

The current owners have restored elements of the original interior design, such as the handpainted Chinese wallpaper in the dining room.

Frank Lloyd Wright designed this passive solar hemicycle house—his second commission from Herbert Jacobs—so that its window walls are oriented to the angles of the sun. The house also demonstrates Wright's shift of interest from rectangular forms to other shapes such as the circle and the triangle, as can also be seen in his 1953 residence Kentuck Knob (see pages 176–8).

Stone was particularly suited to Wright's organic aesthetic, and he built many houses of stone in the 1940s and 1950s. The rough-faced rectangular stones projecting from this house evoke the randomness of nature. Wright reinforced the house's organic qualities by merging

the walls with earth berms so that the structure seems to rise from the ground.

According to Terry L. Patterson, "The property of stone that plays the largest role in the character of Wright's buildings is its form. Its natural blocky mass often established building character and was rarely forced into shapes of unnatural delicacy or precision."[11]

The transparency and lightness of the glass wall that stretches across almost the entire south facade is emphasized by massive stone walls flanking it at either end. Deep eaves reinforce the curve of the structure and provide shade from the sun.

OPPOSITE: The curving window wall, anchored by stone at each end, is oriented to the angles of the sun. Deep eaves not only reinforce the curve of the wall but also provide shade.

ABOVE: Frank Lloyd Wright's organic aesthetic is expressed in the merging of the house's structure with earth berms.

Kentuck Knob   Frank Lloyd Wright   Chalk Hill, Pennsylvania   1953

Frank Lloyd Wright was sixty-eight when he designed Fallingwater, the celebrated weekend house built for Pittsburgh millionaire Edgar J. Kaufmann above Bear Run Falls in Pennsylvania. He was eighty-six in 1953 when he designed Kentuck Knob, another dramatic Pennsylvania mountain retreat seven miles down the road from Fallingwater, for Mr. and Mrs. I. N. Hogan.

By World War I, interest in Wright's Prairie Style houses had faded, at least for the affluent client. For a time, Wright's work was in eclipse. But in the 1930s he reemerged as a major figure in the profession, due in part to the commission for Fallingwater. Wright had reshaped his principles of Prairie architecture, giving his work new vigor and authority. Although he denounced the International Style, its influence can be seen in his designs of both Fallingwater and Kentuck Knob.

Kentuck Knob represents Wright's principles of organic architecture

as refined during his long career. In the intervening years since Fallingwater, Wright had developed an interest in designing with shapes other than the rectangle, such as the hexagon and the circle. He designed Kentuck Knob based on a hexagonal grid of equilateral triangles.

Constructed of local stone, the house appears to rise from its site, jutting out in places to capture vistas and conform to the landscape, folding in at others to provide intimate interior spaces. Stone offered Wright inspiration in its formations, which he found essentially geometric and which, as he said, offered the architect inspiring "marvels of beauty." Indeed, stone inspired Wright throughout his career; during the 1940s and 1950s he designed a great many houses of stone.

The house is owned today by Lord and Lady Peter Palumbo of London, whose decision to open it to tours allows the public to experience directly Wright's continuing virtuosity late in his career.

OPPOSITE: A deep eave with cutouts overhangs the terrace, which mediates between landscape and living space and helps to create a unity of nature and house. The flagstone terrace continues into the floors of the interior.

ABOVE: The house at twilight. The living space and terrace are elevated to capture views, and the cantilevered roof, supported only by two stone piers, appears to float.

The low, broad risers provide a
gracious approach to the entrance,
allowing the visitor to appreciate the
subtle colorations of the stone. Lit
from within, the abstract clerestory
windows glow under the eaves.

The massive angled fireplace serves as
the anchor of the house's living space.

The dining space is an enclosed continuation of the terrace. Designed by Wright, the built-in table extends directly from the sideboard. Its angled shape is in keeping with the hexagonal grid of the house.

The kitchen, with its rough stone walls, is the central core of the house.

Four folding transparent panels at the entrance blur the transition between exterior and interior, as do the field-stone floor and walls. Here sandstone, cypress, and glass come together. This palette of materials is used throughout the house.

Bauhaus architect Marcel Breuer (1902–1981) and his associate Herbert Beckhard (1926–) frequently used stone in the more than thirty houses they built during their twenty-eight-year collaboration. Although they designed great modernist public buildings, they valued their residential work for the opportunity to develop ideas on a small scale, something they could not do in larger projects.

Modern structures are often indifferent to context. Not so with Breuer and Beckhard houses. The architects used local, indigenous materials whenever possible, as they did in the Hooper residence.

The house appears at first not to be a house at all, but simply a stone wall. The entrance, two five-foot-wide sliding glass doors, is cut into 140 feet of an otherwise unbroken expanse of thickly mortared Maryland fieldstones. A long stretch of earth-toned stones in hues of gray and rust, the wall allies itself with its natural surroundings. At once earthbound and sculptural, it demands attention; seldom is stone seen on such a scale or in such a powerful form.

Once through the sliding doors and into a large courtyard, the house's transparency is revealed. To one side, a wall of glass opens to the living room. At the back of the court is another stone wall with a wide rectangular opening, affording a view—or passage—through the entry and court to a lake beyond. The beauty of the stone is further expressed in the thickness of the walls—sixteen inches—which can be seen in the reveals where solid meets void and where stone meets glass.

The court separates the living wing from the sleeping wing in a "binuclear" plan typical of many Breuer designs. The two wings are linked by an enclosed walkway of bluestone flooring. Maryland fieldstone is brought inside to form a wall in the living and dining areas, as well as in two of the bedrooms, thus fusing exterior and interior. Each of the bedrooms has a wall of glass, making the rooms not only seem larger but also blurring the distinction between dwelling and nature. The house, which at first appears to be one low story, is sited on a rise, allowing a lower level for a garage, stables, mechanical equipment, and a staff apartment.

Although the house is large—encompassing 7,800 square feet—it is aesthetically simple, both in plan and in the limited palette of materials. Indeed, the Maryland fieldstone itself is the decoration, and it is all that is needed.

The glass-walled living room. The cutout in the courtyard wall is visible to the left of the living room, and the bedroom wing extends beyond it.

The Maryland fieldstone front of the house—seemingly more wall than house—demands attention to its texture and colors. In spite of its geometry, the wall blends beautifully into its natural surroundings.

Looking through the cutout into the
courtyard opposite the entrance. The
design is a study in contrasts: solid
and void, heavy and light, organic and
man-made.

Transparent walls and stonework serve
to unite interior and exterior.

The house drops down toward the
Arkansas River. The finely laid native
limestone imitates nature in its randomness while also emphasizing the
design's horizontality.

E. Fay Jones, recipient of the 1990 AIA Gold Medal, has said, "I am always pleased to have the opportunity to acknowledge the influence of Frank Lloyd Wright."[12] Jones, however, pursued a path independent of Wright's influence as well as that of Bruce Goff, under whom he had taught at the University of Oklahoma.

In no small way did place play a part in that independence. Jones returned to Arkansas, his birthplace, after teaching and an apprenticeship with Wright at Taliesin. Isolated from peer pressure and the contrasting stylistic currents of the East and West coasts, he was free to pursue his own point of view. He appreciated his inherited principles, believing that architecture is a continuum and that history can serve as a catalyst for ideas. Thus, he drew from his mentors' principles, reinterpreting them to develop an evolving body of work with its own sense of place.

Using nature as a source of inspiration, Jones infused his work with the spirit of organic design, merging the interior with the exterior. The porch's deep, sheltering eaves extend into the landscape. Rooms flow freely into each other with minimal wall separations.

Designed for a career diplomat, Graham Hall, when he retired to his native Little Rock, Pine Knoll appears from the driveway to be a single-story house situated just below the brow of the hill, in keeping with the Wrightian principle that a house should not be *on* the hill, but just below it. The long, low roof seems almost to meet the lawn. A second floor containing guest bedrooms is recessed below the main floor, which overhangs and shelters it. Finely laid limestone emphasizes the horizontality of the house while echoing the natural outcroppings scattered on the hill as it drops down to the Arkansas River. As sited on the bluff, the house originally had expansive river vistas, but the water is now largely obscured by mature trees and plantings. Only when the trees have shed their leaves does the river appear.

Pine Knoll was an important commission that brought E. Fay Jones and his residential designs to the attention of a wider audience. For the present owners, who have meticulously maintained the house with only minor changes to the interiors, it continues to provide comfort and a sense of being at home with nature.

ABOVE: Bedrooms are recessed below the main living floor.

RIGHT: The terrace projects into the wooded site.

The living room's transparent wall
opens to the trees. Jones's signature
cross bracing would evolve in his
work, culminating later in his famous
chapel designs.

The soffit trim and intersecting planes in the galley kitchen recall the work of Frank Lloyd Wright.

The entry's interior atrium contains a garden and pond. A lowered wood ceiling opens to a skylight above.

A reading corner of the living room, with its stone hearth. Appalachian oak panels line the ceiling, which is washed in light from cove fixtures.

CHAPTER 5

TWENTY-FIRST CENTURY

In the year 2002 perhaps it is far too early to predict where domestic architecture will go in the next century. Will the years 2050, 2100, or 3000 for that matter see entirely new forms of shelter?

One can only look at the past and compare it to the present. Styles have changed and yet remained basically the same. While many houses in traditional period revival styles continue to be built, often next door to them are modernist houses. But what does seem to have evolved is a greater freedom of style. The public has become more accepting of different versions of contemporary design and more comfortable with modernism. Chris Coy of Barnes Coy Architects notes that ten years ago ten percent of their work was modern design and ninety percent traditional. Today sixty percent is modern and forty percent traditional. A big sea change. Not only are more modern houses being built, but whereas modern designs used to have smaller budgets and traditional houses larger ones, today that too has changed. Now more money is being spent on contemporary designs than on their traditional counterparts, indicating, Coy believes, that people have more confidence in modern architecture.

Modernism itself has evolved. The orthodox modern house in concrete, glass, and steel standing as an object on the land, rejected by mainstream America as too sterile, has been transformed. For years architects have been experimenting with breaking out of the box. With the aid of the computer, they are able to manipulate abstract forms and volumes, designing houses that appear to break apart, rotate like pinwheels, climb hillsides, or disappear into them. Advances in engineering make it possible for architects to realize these designs. And yet, the rectangular box is still with us, just as it was four hundred years ago. Indeed, the restoration and preservation of historic houses continues to foster appreciation for the country's architectural heritage.

The four architectural firms represented in this chapter are modernist practitioners. They employ modernism's formal strategies of juxtaposing solid and void, openness and enclosure, angle and curve, transparency and opacity. But they use these tactics to respond to the environment, historic and cultural precedents, and technology. Vernacular forms and practices, local materials, and climate are all elements that inform their work. They create designs that are very much of this century by working in the present while drawing on the continuum of the past.

Stone is the material of mountain regions. Three of the houses included in this chapter are in mountain country. The fourth, a Deamer + Phillips design, employs stone in an innovative manner for an oceanside villa. Scott Phillips says he and his partner Peggy Deamer like the challenge of referring to vernacular forms in their modernist designs. On Long Island they have created a house that incorporates a simple rectangular box of wood—a vernacular type common to the area—with stone. They use a stone wall as a counterpoint to the wood shingles, but also in response to climatic and site conditions. The wall's design simplifies and streamlines the composition, giving the house its modernist edge.

Lake/Flato Architects are modernists committed to creating buildings that capture the spirit of place. In stating their philosophy, David Lake and Ted Flato say they create regional designs by looking at context through understanding the culture and architectural history of the region

PREVIOUS PAGE: A stone wall and bentwood railing at the House in the Adirondacks by Bohlin Cywinski Jackson.

and responding sensitively to the site. Furthermore, they believe a building should embrace the latest innovations in technology and sustainability. Daylighting, climatic response, and the use of local materials, craft, and art should imbue a building with its unique character. Their designs are modern yet tactile, environmentally responsible, and inspirational. Lake feels it is increasingly important to connect people to their place, making them part of the larger environment. The firm's work continues the tradition of place-making with a sense of ingenuity, a typically American response to solving problems with what one has at hand that can be traced back to the pioneers.

For the new century Lake and Flato discuss the importance of sustainability in architecture, the tenets of energy-efficient design that advocate building with the least possible impact on the earth and its resources and with minimal transportation. The Green Building Council's standards of sustainable building are difficult, according to Lake, but if adhered to they make buildings more specific to place because they address factors of climate, terrain, and local materials. In the house illustrated here, the architects have brilliantly melded together a modernist aesthetic with the specifics of the site. In doing so, they have created sustainable architecture that will shape the way the occupants live in the house and how they interact with their natural environment.

The firm of Bohlin Cywinski Jackson has gained national recognition for excellence in responding to the unique needs of the client, site, and program, as the house shown in this chapter demonstrates. The architects have reinterpreted the traditional form of the Adirondack great camp in a fresh and innovative manner, using local materials to create a modern vacation house that respects its natural surroundings.

Chris Coy and Rob Barnes have used modernist forms and strategies to design a house that relates to its mountain setting. Its stone gives the house a weight that is the equal of the mountain itself. Discussing residential architecture for the new century, Coy points out that manufacturers continue to develop new materials that change building technology and construction methods. Lumber, for example, is now engineered so that it is stable in all climate conditions, allowing for finer details. Advances in technology also improve how houses function: mechanicals continue to get smaller, taking up less space. In the firm's design shown in this chapter, cutting-edge technology was used to create a superbly functional house that is perfectly suited to its mountainside site.

Traditionally at the head of the hierarchy of building materials, stone has meant status. However, architects are finding more economical ways of employing it, resulting in its wider use. For centuries they have been working in stone to reflect the natural landscape, leaving a legacy of historic works thanks to the durability of the material. Now architects explore the possibilities of the material on its own terms, finding inventive ways to counterbalance the object on the land with that in the land. Even in the most abstract designs, stone evokes its natural origins, giving an organic presence to manmade structure. That is the charisma of stone.

This Castle Rock, Colorado, house takes its inspiration from a photograph of a burial cairn in Ireland. Architect David Lake of the San Antonio firm of Lake/Flato showed the image to his clients, saying, "The house should feel like this, part of the land." They had shown him a picture of quite a different form, a Roman arcade. But they were soon convinced that he was right.

The site chosen, a rocky hillside with expansive views of the Front Range, seemed suited to a structure that would disappear into the slope rather than rise as an arcade. Lake/Flato's scheme rooted the house into the site, making it an integral part of the landscape. Huge boulders anchor rustic granite walls that recall the ruins of Mesa Verde and Chaco Canyon. The boulders' presence make the house "feel more particular to its place," Lake says.

The house has a low profile from the road. To reach it, one crosses a flat mesa and then descends along a sloping walkway contained by stone walls. Inside, the house is divided into two wings. To the left is the private master wing containing the kitchen, family room, master bedroom, and office. The east-facing bedrooms burrow about twelve feet into the hillside and have close views into natural arroyo courtyards. Sod roofs cover these rooms, merging the house with the land, while in other sections of the house roofs take the vernacular shed form reminiscent of rusty minehead shacks, an allusion to the state's mining past.

Contrasting with the intimate, stone-enclosed private quarters, a public wing containing the living room and dining room opens to expansive views. A north-south gallery links the west-facing public pavilions, which perch like great glass bay windows over the steep site. The volumes are rotated along the site's edge, their views oriented to individual mountain peaks. The dialogue between heavy stone and light steel and glass occurs throughout the house.

Sliding pocket doors and stone floors without thresholds lead to outdoor terraces, integrating the house with nature and fulfilling the clients' desire for a seamless interchange between inside and outside. The architects' palette of sandstone, granite, and copper with a natural patina echoes the colors of the landscape.

It is perhaps surprising that such a stunning modern structure of steel and glass should integrate so well with its site. Yet, as Lake says, "People driving by would not even know the house was there."

ABOVE: The terrace overlooks a view of the Front Range.

OPPOSITE: At the entrance, rustic granite walls anchored by boulders rise from the hillside, recalling the ruins of Mesa Verde and Chaco Canyon. The metal roofs are reminiscent of Colorado's vernacular mining sheds.

SITE/FLOOR PLAN

PREVIOUS SPREAD: The steel-and-glass living pavilion perches like a great bay window over the steep site. Its transparency contrasts with the enclosure of the house's private rooms. The six-foot-wide overhangs of the standing-seam copper roof, low-emissivity glass, and window shades reduce the heat load and control glare.

ABOVE: Integrally colored plaster walls and oak cabinetry complement the pale floors and lavatory of Colorado sandstone.

The east-facing bedrooms are dug
into the hillside with close views into
courtyards. Sod covers their roofs,
eliminating the need for cooling.

ABOVE: Walls of local granite flow in and out of the house, while the sandstone floors echo the colors of the natural environment.

OPPOSITE: Granite boulders surround the swimming pool, into which water flows as if it were a natural arroyo. Native grasses and flowers grow among the rocky outcroppings. The house maintains a low profile to the site.

Not many of the early-twentieth-century great camps of the Adirondacks are left today, but the charm of their rustic architecture lives on. Drawing on such vernacular forms as Swiss chalets and Stick Style villas, the Adirondack style is distinguished from other traditions by its use of un-milled logs for columns, giant boulders, and handcrafted twig furniture.

The clients, a couple with a young family, asked Bohlin Cywinski Jackson of Wilkes-Barre, Pennsylvania, to bring some of the feeling of the great camps to their own weekend retreat overlooking an Adirondack Mountain lake in upstate New York. The architects were careful in siting the building in the landscape to preserve its wooded character and take maximum advantage of sun and views. The clients preferred to sacrifice bedroom and bathroom size in order to devote most of the four thousand square feet, to which the dwelling was limited by code, to communal spaces. The steep slope of the site facing the lake to the southeast allowed a full lower floor to be constructed below the entry floor. This became the domain of the children.

A massive stone fireplace dominates the central living space, its stacked granite boulders providing hearths for the master bedroom and lower-level playroom as well. The modernist grid of the window wall opens the living space to sun and views. Architect Peter Bohlin points out that the house's modernist free plan differs from the conventional rectangular rooms of the traditional camps. In the living space, columns are shifted away from the structural bays, giving an impression of randomness rather like the trees of the surrounding forest. The entry axis of the cross-shaped plan is shifted at an angle, and two wings containing bedrooms and baths extend from the central section. A screened porch extends out toward the forest and lake on the opposite side of the house.

The stone base of the house, the tree-columns, and the rustic stick work establish a dialogue with the forest. The architects have respected the natural environment while responding to the unique needs of the clients and the site, evoking, through a modernist interpretation, the essence of Adirondack great camps.

LEFT: Columns and beams of massive tree trunks, a hearth of giant boulders, and furniture fashioned from natural branches and twigs echo the interiors of the Adirondack great camps.

OPPOSITE: Tree-columns contrast with the transparency of the entrance gable. Carefully placed boulders mark the transition between the natural and the human-made.

ABOVE: The roof planes and stone chimney are visible through the pine and hemlock forest. The lead-coated copper roof softly reflects the sky.

OPPOSITE: Enormous granite boulders form the fireplace.

SITE PLAN

0 10 20   40   80

The house is an extension of the
forest, its stone base rising out of
the hillside.

Red pine-bark siding and rustic stick work forming the balusters engage in a dialogue with the surroundings. The lower level contains the children's playroom and bedrooms.

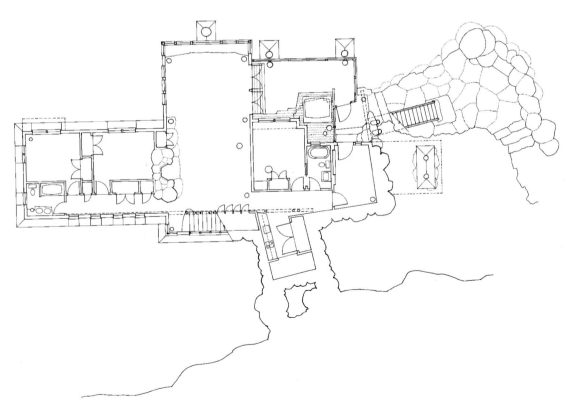

The owner of this residence, located on a steep bluff overlooking the Atlantic Ocean, wanted a house that would recall the stone building tradition of his native Basque region in Spain. In addition, the building code placed limitations on the length and height of the house. Thus, the architects, Scott Phillips and Peggy Deamer of New York City, were given the challenge of accommodating these requirements in their design.

They felt that a house of permeable stone did not make sense facing wind-driven salt air. Instead, they designed a simple rectangular wood-frame house, all of its rooms facing the view (also a client request). A thick, dry-stacked stone wall wraps around two sides of the house away from the view. The wall serves to brace the lighter wood structure against ocean winds while also retaining the steep hill behind the house and baffling sounds from the road. Finally, by pulling the wall away from the house, the architects broke the formality of the rectangular box. The void between the stone wall and the house is skylit and contains the entry stair. To provide roof access, also requested by the client, a fully

glazed dining room angles off the southeast corner of the residence, yielding a roof deck off the master bedroom. A copper roof—rather than shingle—allowed a lower pitch (meeting code height requirements) while simplifying and streamlining the form, giving the whole composition a sleek appearance.

Building code also forced the swimming pool to be moved from the bluff, the original intention, and located at the front of the house, where the stone wall forms an edge. Downspouts are cut in the face of the stone to channel water into the pool. A guest house built closer to the road shields the pool, giving it privacy.

Scott Phillips says that he and his partner like the challenge of incorporating vernacular elements in their work. "Most clients," he says, "have a vernacular imagery in mind when they come to us." Deamer + Phillips's designs reinterpret traditional forms with a modernist point of view.

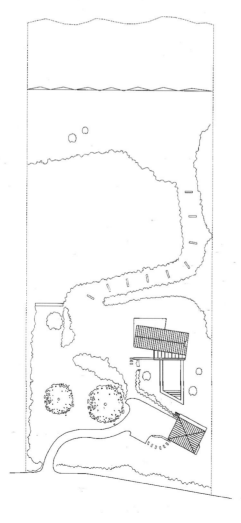

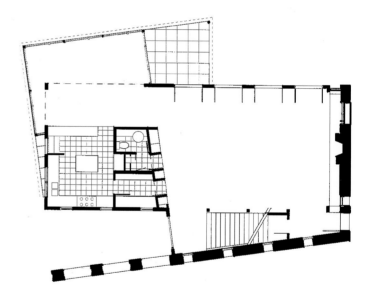

OPPOSITE: A thick, dry-stacked stone wall, pulled away from the house, retains the steep hill and braces the lighter wood-frame house against ocean winds. Downspouts cut into the face of the stone channel water into the swimming pool. The regular grid of the windows reflects the architects' modernist vocabulary, while the low pitch of the roof and the sparely detailed stone wall make a sleek composition.

OPPOSITE: The entrance fills the void between the stone wall and the frame house.

The entrance foyer is skylit and contains the stairway.

The glass-enclosed dining room and kitchen provide spectacular views of the ocean.

ABOVE: A 1,200-square-foot guest house with stone piers is sited closer to the road, shielding the pool area and providing privacy.

OPPOSITE: The stone wall breaks the formality of the box. Fulfilling the client's request, it is a modernist expression of a vernacular form—that of the stone buildings of his native Basque region of Spain.

Architects Chris Coy and Robert Barnes of Bridgehampton, New York, believe that the necessities of site and context are very useful in directing design.

Here, for example, in this house in Colorado ski country, snow load dictated the design of the roofs. The standing-seam copper roofs of the various pavilions employ barrel, prismatic, and pitched shapes to shed snow, while hot water and glycol encased in concrete in the roofs aid in melting snow accumulation.

Echoing the surrounding mountains, the forms of the house juxtapose angles and curves. A double-height window-wall opens the house to a spectacular mountain view, while its transparency and lightness are emphasized by the massive stone walls. Also responding to the mountain context are the house's materials—monumental tree-columns footed on stone bases and stone rubble. For the columns, the architects imported from Calgary, Canada, thirteen dead-standing cedar trees, half petrified in the arctic air. Twelve of the trees are twenty to twenty-four feet tall and are used as structural columns. The thirteenth, fifty-two feet long by three feet in diameter, supports the ridge of the house and is expressed at the peak of the rear gable. For the rusticated, rubble stone walls, the

designers purchased four thousand tons of moss rock from a rancher's outcropping in southeastern Colorado. The stone cut and stacked well, and it was laid so that no joints would show. Huge pieces of stone—seven and fourteen feet—were used for the lintels. No mere veneer, these stone walls are eighteen inches thick, giving the house enough weight to match the mountain.

A previous house on the property was torn down. The local building code required that all that was taken down be put back and no more. So, although the house is replete with up-to-date elements, it is no larger than the one that preceded it. All voids are taken up with the wiring so that mechanical systems are integrated with the structure. The basement houses a computer that enables the owners to operate many of the residence's mechanical functions by remote control.

The various rooms are sited to accommodate the terrain and take advantage of different views. The materials make the house at home with its mountain setting and the surrounding landscape. With its inventive design and state-of-the-art technological features, the house epitomizes architecture of the twenty-first century.

Transparency is juxtaposed with the solidity of the stone walls. The dining table is a single three-inch slab of African mahogany. The balustrade stickwork imitates tree branches.

The double-height window-wall opens
the back of the house and dining
area to majestic mountain views.
Monumental tree columns of dead-
standing cedars imported from
Calgary, Canada, support the gable.
The ridgepole that extends the length
of the house—three feet in diameter
and fifty-two feet long—is seen at
the apex of the gable.

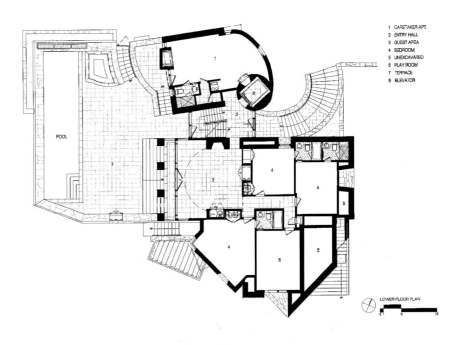

1 CARETAKER APT.
2 ENTRY HALL
3 GUEST AREA
4 BEDROOM
5 UNEXCAVATED
6 PLAY ROOM
7 TERRACE
8 ELEVATOR

LOWER FLOOR PLAN

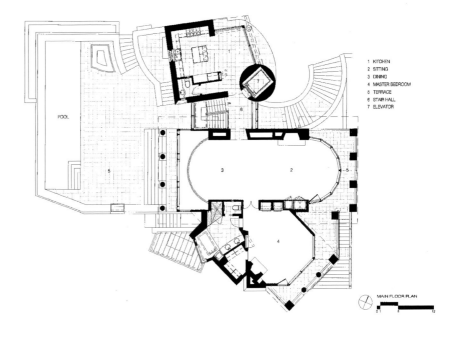

1 KITCHEN
2 SITTING
3 DINING
4 MASTER BEDROOM
5 TERRACE
6 STAIR HALL
7 ELEVATOR

MAIN FLOOR PLAN

LEFT: The front of the house. The entrance is located in the glass bay between the stone pavilions. The various pavilions of the house employ barrel, prismatic, and pitched roofs to shed snow.

Ruin-like rusticated stone walls contrast with the sleekness of the modern kitchen. The flooring is of Colorado sandstone.

Colorado moss rock surrounds the master-bedroom fireplace.

The barrel-vaulted section of the
house contains the master bedroom.

Notes

INTRODUCTION

1. Frank Lloyd Wright, "In the Cause of Architecture: III. The Meaning of Materials—Stone," in Hugh S. Donlan and Martin Filler, eds., *In the Cause of Architecture: Wright's Historic Essays for* Architectural Record, *1908–1952* (New York: McGraw-Hill, 1987), 172.
2. Ibid., 173.
3. Ibid., 171.

CHAPTER 2

1. Quoted in John Milnes Baker, A.I.A., *American House Styles: A Concise Guide* (New York: W. W. Norton & Co., 1994), 18.
2. Leland M. Roth, *A Concise History of American Architecture* (New York: Icon Editions, Harper & Row, 1979), 13–14.
3. Harley J. McKee, *Introduction to Early American Masonry: Stone, Brick, Mortar, and Plaster* (Washington, D.C.: Preservation Press, 1973), 9–15 passim.
4. Helen Wilkinson Reynolds, *Dutch Houses in the Hudson Valley Before 1776* (Payson and Clark, 1929; rpt. New York: Dover, 1965), 11–22 passim.
5. National Park Service, "Dutch Colonies," www.cr.nps.gov, updated 4/25/2000.
6. Reynolds, 178.
7. Ibid., 179.
8. Ibid., 19.
9. National Park Service.
10. Wendell Garrett, *American Colonial: Puritan Simplicity to Georgian Grace* (New York: Monacelli Press), 1995, 126–28.
11. Baker, 44.
12. Carole Rifkind, *A Field Guide to American Architecture* (New York: New American Library, 1980), 29.

CHAPTER 3

1. Quoted in Leland M. Roth, ed., *America Builds* (New York: Harper & Row, 1983), 157.
2. Rifkind, 38.
3. William H. Pierson, Jr., *Technology and the Picturesque: The Corporate and Early Gothic Styles,* vol. 2 of *American Buildings and Their Architects* (New York: Oxford University Press, 1978), 4–21 passim.
4. Ibid., 6.
5. Ibid., 10.
6. A. J. Downing, *The Architecture of Country Houses*, quoted in Pierson, 349–50.
7. Ibid., 408.
8. Quoted in Vincent J. Scully Jr., *The Shingle Style and the Stick Style: Architectural Theory and Design from Downing to the Origins of Wright*, rev. ed. (New Haven: Yale University Press, 1971), xxxiii.
9. Pierson, 408.
10. John Zukowsky, *Hudson River Villas* (New York: Rizzoli, 1985), 11.
11. Charles J. Plante II, "The Deshon–Allyn House, New London, Connecticut," *Antiques Magazine* (Oct. 1986).
12. Pierson, 332.
13. Scully, 92.
14. Quoted in Scully, 92.
15. Ibid.
16. Virginia and Lee McAlester, *Great American Houses and Their Architectural Styles* (New York: Abbeville Press, 1994), 178–89 passim.
17. Ibid.
18. Mark Alan Hewitt, *The Architect of the American Country House, 1890–1940* (New Haven: Yale University Press, 1990), 128.

CHAPTER 4

1. Roth, *A Concise History of American Architecture,* 231.
2. Ibid., chapter 6, passim.
3. Ibid., 232.
4. Mark Alan Hewitt, "The Other Proper Style," *Old House Journal* (April 1997): 30 passim.
5. William Jordy, *The Impact of European Modernism in the Mid-Twentieth Century*, vol. 5 of *American Buildings and Their Architects* (New York: Oxford University Press, 1972), 169–70; see also Christopher Wilk, *Marcel Breuer: Furniture and Interiors* (New York: Museum of Modern Art, 1981), 142.
6. McAlester, 268 passim.
7. Charles Miller, "The James House," *Fine Homebuilding* (Dec. 1984/Jan. 1985).
8. Linda Leigh Paul, *Cottages by the Sea: The Handmade Homes of Carmel, America's First Artist Community* (New York: Universe, 2000), 16–26 passim., 48–53.
9. Dale Mulfinger, *The Architecture of Edwin Lundie* (Minneapolis: Minnesota Historical Society Press, 1995).
10. City of Lake Forest, Illinois, Historic Resources Survey, Statement of Significance.
11. Terry L. Patterson, *Frank Lloyd Wright and the Meaning of Materials* (New York: Van Nostrand Reinhold, 1994), 81.
12. Quoted in Robert Adams Ivy, *Fay Jones* (Washington, D.C.: American Institute of Architects Press, 1992), 23.

SELECTED BIBLIOGRAPHY

BOOKS

Allport, Susan. *Sermons in Stone: The Stone Walls of New England and New York.* New York: W. W. Norton & Co., 1990.

Baker, John Milnes. *American House Styles: A Concise Guide.* New York: W. W. Norton & Co., 1994.

Bracken, Dorothy Kendall, and Maurine Whorton Redway. *Early Texas Homes.* Dallas: Southern Methodist University Press, 1956.

Carley, Rachel. *The Visual Dictionary of American Domestic Architecture.* New York: Henry Holt & Co., 1994.

Clark, Clifford Edward, Jr., *The American Family Home, 1800–1960.* Chapel Hill: University of North Carolina Press, 1986.

De Long, David G., Helen Searing, and Robert A. M. Stern, eds. *American Architecture: Innovation and Tradition.* New York: Rizzoli, 1986.

Frasch, Robert W., Olaf William Shelgren Jr., and Cary Lattin. *Cobblestone Landmarks of New York State.* Syracuse: Syracuse University Press, 1978.

Garrett, Wendell. *American Colonial: Puritan Simplicity to Georgian Grace.* New York: Monacelli Press, 1995.

Hewitt, Mark Alan. *The Architect and the American Country House, 1890–1940.* New Haven: Yale University Press, 1990.

Hyman, Isabelle. *Marcel Breuer, Architect: The Career and the Buildings.* New York: Harry N. Abrams, Inc., 2001.

Ivy, Robert Adams. *Fay Jones.* Washington, D.C.: American Institute of Architects Press, 1992.

Jordy, William H. *Progressive and Academic Ideals at the Turn of the Twentieth Century.* Vol. 4, *American Buildings and Their Architects.* New York: Oxford University Press, 1972.

_____. *The Impact of European Modernism in the Mid-Twentieth Century.* Vol. 5, *American Buildings and Their Architects.* New York: Oxford University Press, 1972.

Keefe, Charles S., ed. *The American House, Being a Collection of Illustrations & Plans of the Best Country & Suburban Houses Built in the United States during the Last Few Years.* New York: U.P.C. Book Company, 1922.

Massey, James C., and Shirley Maxwell. *House Styles in America.* New York: Penguin Studio, 1996.

McAlester, Virginia and Lee. *Great American Houses and Their Architectural Styles.* New York: Abbeville Press, 1994.

McGrew, Patrick, and Robert Julian. *Landmarks of Los Angeles.* New York: Harry N. Abrams, Inc., 1994.

McKee, Harley J. *Introduction to Early American Masonry: Stone, Brick, Mortar, and Plaster.* Washington, D.C.: Preservation Press, 1973.

Mulfinger, Dale. *The Architecture of Edwin Lundie.* Minneapolis: Minnesota Historical Society Press, 1995.

Noble, Allen G. *Wood, Brick, and Stone.* Amherst: University of Massachusetts Press, 1984.

O'Gorman, James F. *Three American Architects: Richardson, Sullivan, and Wright, 1865–1915.* Chicago: University of Chicago Press, 1991.

Patterson, Terry L. *Frank Lloyd Wright and the Meaning of Materials.* New York: Van Nostrand Reinhold, 1994.

Paul, Linda Leigh. *Cottages by the Sea: The Handmade Homes of Carmel, America's First Artist Community.* New York: Universe, 2000.

Pearson, Clifford A., ed. *Modern American Houses: Four Decades of Award-Winning Design in* Architectural Record. New York: Harry N. Abrams, Inc., 1996.

Pierson, William H., Jr. *The Colonial and Neoclassical Styles.* Vol. 1, *American Buildings and Their Architects.* New York: Oxford University Press, 1970.

_____. *Technology and the Picturesque: The Corporate and the Early Gothic Styles.* Vol. 2, *American Buildings and Their Architects.* New York: Oxford University Press, 1978.

Quiney, Anthony. *The Traditional Buildings of England.* London: Thames and Hudson, 1990.

Reynolds, Helen Wilkinson. *Dutch Houses in the Hudson Valley Before 1776.* Payson and Clark for the Holland Society of New York, 1929; rpt. New York: Dover, 1965.

Rifkind, Carole. *A Field Guide to American Architecture.* New York: New American Library, 1980.

Roth, Leland M. *A Concise History of American Architecture.* New York: Icon Editions, Harper & Row, 1979.

_____, ed. *America Builds.* New York: Harper & Row, 1983.

Sanders, Scott R. *Stone Country.* Bloomington: Indiana University Press, 1985.

Schmidt, Carl F. *Cobblestone Masonry.* Scottsville, N.Y., 1966.

Scully, Vincent J., Jr. *The Shingle Style and the Stick Style: Architectural Theory and Design from Downing to the Origins of Wright.* Rev. ed. New Haven: Yale University Press, 1971.

_____. *The Shingle Style Today or the Historian's Revenge.* New York: George Braziller, 1974.

Upton, Dell, and John Michael Vlach, eds. *Common Places: Readings in American Vernacular Architecture.* Athens, Ga.: University of Georgia Press, 1986.

Wilk, Christopher. *Marcel Breuer: Furniture and Interiors.* New York: Museum of Modern Art, 1981.

Williams, Henry Lionel, and Ottalie K. Williams. *A Guide to Old American Houses 1700–1900.* New York: A. S. Barnes and Co., 1962.

Winkler, E. M. *Stone in Architecture: Properties, Durability.* 3rd ed. Berlin: Springer-Verlag, 1994.

Wright, Frank Lloyd. *In the Cause of Architecture: Wright's Historic Essays for Architectural Record, 1908–1952.* Hugh S. Donlan and Martin Filler, eds. New York: McGraw-Hill, 1975, 1987.

Wright, Richardson, ed. *House & Garden's Second Book of Houses.* New York: Conde Nast Publications, 1925.

Zukowsky, John. *Hudson River Villas.* New York: Rizzoli, 1985.

ARTICLES

Bock, Gordon. "Stone Houses." *Old House Journal* (July–Aug. 1991).

Friedberg, M. Paul. "Random Thoughts on Stone." *Building Stone Magazine* (Jan.–Feb. 1989).

Hewitt, Mark Alan. "The Other Proper Style: Tudor Revival, 1880–1940." *Old House Journal* (April 1997).

Keister, Kim. "History Lesson: Samuel Chew's Cliveden." *Historic Preservation* (Nov.–Dec. 1993).

Miller, Charles. "The James House." *Fine Homebuilding* (Dec. 1984/Jan. 1985).

ACKNOWLEDGMENTS

Many people contributed their enthusiasm, knowledge, cooperation, and support to the making of this work. Without their assistance the book would not have been possible; I thank all those who were so very helpful.

Museum, historical society, and planning department officials were particularly helpful, giving their time to talk to me and provide suggestions and history. Some had contributed information for my earlier book on contemporary stone houses. I was able to draw on that as well as new research for the present work. My gratitude goes to Blanca Materne of the Gillespie County Historical Society in Fredericksburg, Texas; Catherine Andrews and Irene Epstein of Lyndhurst; Meg Schaefer of the von Hess Foundation, which owns Wright's Ferry Mansion; Peter Coutant of the City of Lake Forest Planning Department; David Wolner of the Roosevelt Institute, and Sarah Olsen and Ann Jordan of the National Park Service, all of whom helped with the Roosevelt properties; William Maurer, director of the Gomez Mill House; Susan Waggoner, director of Kentuck Knob; Peter Latham of the Chestnut Hill Historical Society; John Braunlein and Leslie LeFevre-Stratton of the Huguenot Historical Society; Susan DiCicco of the James House; Constance Weissmuller of the Robinson Jeffers house; Marie O'Neill of the Ebenezer Maxwell Mansion; Michael McBride, curator of the Henry Whitfield State Museum; Jayne Swantner of Oakland House and the Afton, Missouri Historical Society; Delia Robinson and Bill Lattin of the Cobblestone Society Museum in Childs, New York; Esley Hamilton of the Saint Louis County Department of Parks & Recreation; Ken Story of the Arkansas Historic Preservation Program; Phillip Seitz of Cliveden; and Larrie Curry of the Centre Family Dwelling. I am greatly indebted to them all.

Several individuals were especially helpful. Mrs. Edwin Cromey of Tuxedo Park graciously took the time to give me a tour of the park and to provide an introduction to homeowners and arrange for permission to photograph. I thank her for her favors, interest, and kindness. The architect Dale Mulfinger provided information about Edwin Lundie and his houses, about which he has written a book. Bruce Smith gave guidance to the houses of Carmel, as did Robert Judson Clark, Clare McClure, and Enid Sales. Interior designer Lars Bolander and realtor Jim McCann of Sotheby's gave me leads to coquina stone houses in Palm Beach. Although logistical issues did not permit me to include any of their suggestions, I am grateful for their interest. Margaret Pearson and Edwin Ford contributed historical information about Kingston, New York. Architect David McKee located names of present owners of Fay Jones's houses. To all of them I convey my appreciation.

I also express profound gratitude to the architectural firms Barnes Coy, Bohlin Cywinski Jackson, Deamer + Phillips, and Lake/Flato for supplying information and photographs of their contemporary stone designs, which appear in the last chapter of the book and provide a stunning and fitting ending.

I convey my appreciation to the private homeowners who graciously allowed their houses and the interiors to be photographed and included in the book. They contributed immeasurably to this work.

I owe special indebtedness to Elisa Urbanelli for her expert editorial guidance, suggestions, and enthusiastic support.

Finally, my thanks to family and friends for their tolerant patience and belief in my work, which helped to see me through.

EDITOR: Elisa Urbanelli
DESIGNER: Miko McGinty
PRODUCTION COORDINATOR: Maria Pia Gramaglia

Library of Congress Cataloging-in-Publication Data
Goff, Lee.
  Stone houses : colonial to contemporary / text by Lee Goff ; principal
photography by Paul Rocheleau.
     p. cm.
Includes index.
  ISBN 0–8109–3287–3
  1. Architecture, Domestic—United States. 2. Stone houses—United
States. I. Title.
  NA7205 .G57 2002
  728'.37'0973—dc21
                        200200514

Published in 2002 by Harry N. Abrams, Incorporated, New York

Printed and bound in Italy
10 9 8 7 6 5 4 3 2 1

Harry N. Abrams, Inc.
100 Fifth Avenue
New York, N.Y. 10011
www.abramsbooks.com

Abrams is a subsidiary of
🐺 LA MARTINIÈRE
       GROUPE